THEY ARE FEW

POETRY FOR THE MANY

POETRY
FOR THE
MANY

JEREMY CORBYN
AND
LEN McCLUSKEY

OR Books
New York · London

All royalties from the sales of this book will be donated to the Peace and Justice Project. More information at www.thecorbynproject.com.

© 2023 Jeremy Corbyn and Len McCluskey

Published by OR Books, New York and London

Visit our website: www.orbooks.com

Every effort has been made to obtain permission for copyrighted work. Rights queries can be directed to rights@orbooks.com.

All rights reserved. No part of this book may be reproduced or transmitted in any form or by any means, electronic or mechanical, including photocopy, recording, or any information storage retrieval system, without permission in writing from the publisher, except brief passages for review purposes.

First printing 2023

Library of Congress Cataloging-in-Publication Data: A catalog record for this book is available from the Library of Congress.

British Library Cataloging-in-Publication Data: A catalog record for this book is available from the British Library.

Typeset by Lapiz Digital Services. Printed by CPI, UK.

hardback ISBN 978-1-68219-433-1 • ebook ISBN 978-1-68219-434-8

This book is dedicated to all those suffering from miscarriages of justice. In particular, we extend our solidarity to Julian Assange.

CONTENTS

Foreword—*Melissa Benn*	1
Introduction—*Karie Murphy*	3
There's a Poet in All of Us—*Jeremy Corbyn*	9
Poetry Is Food for the Soul—*Len McCluskey*	11

I Wandered Lonely as a Cloud
WILLIAM WORDSWORTH — 13

If—
RUDYARD KIPLING — 15

Remember
CHRISTINA ROSSETTI — 19

The Foggy Dew
CHARLES O'NEILL — 21

Let Me Die a Youngman's Death
ROGER McGOUGH — 24

The Masque of Anarchy (excerpt)
PERCY BYSSHE SHELLEY — 27

In Jerusalem
MAHMOUD DARWISH — 29

I Into History, Now (excerpt)
ANDREW SALKEY — 32

The Negro Speaks of Rivers
LANGSTON HUGHES — 36

Jerusalem ("And did those feet in ancient time")
WILLIAM BLAKE   38

The Tree Council
MIKE JENKINS   41

Invictus
WILLIAM ERNEST HENLEY   45

The Schoolboy
WILLIAM BLAKE   48

The Lark Ascending
GEORGE MEREDITH   51

Do not go gentle into that good night
DYLAN THOMAS   57

A Far Cry from Africa
DEREK WALCOTT   60

Sonnet to Liberty
OSCAR WILDE   63

You Foolish Men
SOR JUANA INÉS DE LA CRUZ   66

"Hope" is the thing with feathers, The Road Not Taken
EMILY DICKINSON and ROBERT FROST   71

Dulce et Decorum Est
WILFRED OWEN   74

Dead Man's Dump
ISAAC ROSENBERG   77

Ballad of a Bushman
WENDELL BROWN   82

For Whom the Bell Tolls
JOHN DONNE 86

sorrow song
LUCILLE CLIFTON 88

The Runaway Slave at Pilgrim's Point
ELIZABETH BARRETT BROWNING 91

Home
WARSAN SHIRE 102

His Hands Were Gentle
ADRIAN MITCHELL 105

Bread and Roses
JAMES OPPENHEIM 109

Scotland, You're No Mine
HANNAH LAVERY 112

Various Love Poems
SHELLEY, BYRON, GIBRAN, YEATS, and SHAKESPEARE 115

The Incandescence of the Wind
BEN OKRI 123

Scots Wha Hae
ROBERT BURNS 128

A Prison Daybreak
FAIZ AHMED FAIZ 131

Death of a Financier
STEVIE SMITH 134

You Are (To My Sons)
ANTONIO GUERRERO RODRÍGUEZ 136

Der fremder in der fremd
IRENA KLEPFISZ   138

Greetings to the People of Europe!
ALEMU TEBEJE   141

The International, The Volunteer
CLIVE BRANSON and CECIL DAY LEWIS   144

The Jumper
CAROLINE SMITH   148

Strange Fruit
ABEL MEEROPOL   153

Say Not the Struggle Nought Availeth
ARTHUR HUGH CLOUGH   155

From Moss Side: For Morris
CARLA HENRY   160

Like a Life-Giving Sun
HAFIZ   164

The Peat Bog Soldiers
JOHANN ESSER and WOLFGANG LANGHOFF   166

Peterloo: Estimated Wrap 19.30
KATE RUTTER   169

Please Call Me by My True Names
THICH NHAT HANH   171

The Horses
EDWIN MUIR   176

More Time
LINTON KWESI JOHNSON   179

Welling
HANNAH LOWE   183

Free Flight
JUNE JORDAN   186

Warning
JENNY JOSEPH   192

Calais in Winter
JEREMY CORBYN   195

Contributors   **199**

Permissions   **205**

Foreword

Melissa Benn

Some might question the connection between politics and poetry. Others will more easily grasp the natural link between the two. As John F Kennedy observed in 1956: 'If more politicians knew poetry and more poets knew politics, I am convinced the world would be a little better place in which to live'.

Poetry jolts us alive somehow. Often a poem can be profoundly moving without us fully understanding exactly what the words on the page—or the silences between them—are doing. Like music, poetry can stir the emotions at some deeper level beneath the conscious. A poem can be subtle, even sly; passionate or downright furious. It can inspire or illuminate a particular moment or movement. A poem can sometimes take a sideways look at human dilemmas or tragedies, or make us laugh in the most unexpected of ways; it can remind us of who we love, and exactly how and why. A poem that captures an event of great significance serves as a historical record of sorts.

In this volume, you will find the work of some of the greatest poets of the last few centuries, selected by a group of individuals who have themselves made a significant contribution to our contemporary political and cultural life. Poetry is not required to submit itself to a collective mandate; even when it directly addresses a political issue, the form enables an authenticity and originality that political life, with its increasingly technocratic calculations, so often lacks. (There are exceptions, of course: those rare orators, like Martin Luther King Jr, who could address a crowd in powerful cadences and with lyrical exactness.)

I hope that this volume not only stands as an introduction to some wonderful poetry but also gives a sense of the rich cultural hinterland of the Left. Here are poems addressing the cruelty and hypocrisy of war, imperialism, racism, and misogyny. Every political and social movement is forever adopting fresh shapes and strategies—for nothing stands still, in either art or politics—but many of the poems mark powerful staging posts in the centuries-long struggle for a more just and humane world.

This collection also gives us the chance to appreciate the choices and commentaries of contributors who have, in markedly different ways, campaigned for social justice and championed the voices of those who have been marginalised, misrepresented, or shot down. Very often, they in turn have been sidelined, mocked, or castigated for their efforts. Within these pages, however, they speak to us unmediated of the experiences and words that have motivated, moved, amused, or enlivened them. In doing so, they take a step towards closing the gap between politics and poetry and help make the world a 'better place in which to live'.

Introduction

Karie Murphy

It's October 2021 and a large crowd is packed into the iconic CASA club in Liverpool—home of the celebrated striking dock workers of the 1990s. The event is a political meeting, but one with a difference. The room is heaving. Some people are standing, some sitting on the floor; most are young and enthused. Not a typical political meeting at all. The proceedings last just ninety minutes, but when they are over it takes another hour and a half for the room to empty. It is a gathering full of positivity and hope. On the stage is a trio of stalwarts of the Left: Jeremy Corbyn, Len McCluskey, and Melissa Benn. And the rallying call of this unusual event? Poetry.

The Politics and Poetry event at the CASA was the springboard for assembling this book. I spoke to a New York resident (originally from Merseyside) in the audience that evening, the publisher Colin Robinson, and out of our discussion came the idea of capturing the mood of that night and blending it with political activism and poetry in a book.

Jeremy and Len, the former leaders of the Labour Party and Unite the Union, are well-known to anyone in Britain with an interest in politics—and to many further afield as well. It's fair to say that neither man fares well in the reporting of a mainstream media in thrall to vested interests.

They are better known and understood on the political Left and among working-class communities, where their values and beliefs are represented more fairly. Both are revered and loved across those communities.

The two men are staunch defenders of democracy, having served in elected positions over the last fifty years. They are both widely-respected public servants, in the real sense of the term. They are unashamedly proud trade unionists who share a common history of fighting injustice in the workplace and their communities.

They are also prominent socialists and internationalists, joining forces over many decades with others who campaign for peace and justice. Branded as anti-establishment figures, they wear the accusation as a badge of honour, taking the view that if the establishment is attacking them, they must be doing something right.

Jeremy is the popular member of Parliament for Islington North, an unrivalled campaigner, widely appreciated for his tenacity, unbending principles, and incorruptibility.

As leader of the Labour Party from 2015 to 2019, he built up the largest-ever membership of any European political party. He changed the face of politics, inspiring millions of young people and those previously written off and marginalised.

Born into a comfortable house in Shropshire, Jeremy benefitted at a young age from being exposed to books and encouraged to read. So began his lifelong love of poetry. His parents were gentle people, active in the anti-racism movement and dedicated to educating their sons on the evils of fascism and colonialism.

Those are principles that Jeremy has never lost and has fought to defend over a lifetime of activism. A true internationalist, he commands global respect. And his experience is reflected in his choice of poetry.

As chief of staff to Jeremy when he led the Labour opposition, I experienced firsthand the qualities that made him a new kind of leader, one who inspired hundreds of thousands of people to actively engage in politics, many for the first time in their lives.

What he offered as a leader was unique. The country had never before seen the sort of rock-star popularity that built up around him, a result of his ability to empower and speak directly to young people, in direct contrast with more conventional politicians who are often seen as out of touch and irrelevant. Jeremy offered that most powerful and life-sustaining of emotions: hope.

Len was, until 2021, the first general secretary of the powerful 'fighting-back union', Unite, known for its global solidarity, its strong political voice, and effective organising in the workplace.

Len's industrial and political savvy stood him apart from other leaders of his era. Under his leadership Unite became the wealthiest and most influential union in the country.

Born in the backstreets of Liverpool, his home was full of love and laughter. Storytelling and singing abounded, but books were a luxury and in short supply. Len was educated, in his words, 'on the Liverpool docks'. It was there that he was politicised, but at the same time he became aware of the many local writers and performers who inspired him with their art and music.

A child of the 1960s and a pupil of the beat scene in Liverpool, he embraced the cultural revolution that was happening around him in his much-loved city.

His experiences later in life would lead him to show support for many people-powered revolutions around the world, where ordinary people fought for fairness, justice, and a better life. Known for his combative style, Len offered workers in struggle what they need most from a leader: confidence.

This book will give the reader a new opportunity to get to know both these men better in a unique and perhaps surprising way. Alongside the widely known fact of their shared political beliefs, there is something less well-known that they have in common and that underpins their friendship: a love of poetry.

In reading *Poetry for the Many*, you will journey through a rich selection of their favourite verse and hear from Jeremy and Len in their own words as they describe how they came across each poem and the impact it had on them. At the same time, they will encourage you, the reader, to embrace poetry and shake off any notion that it is not something to be read, written, or appreciated by working-class people.

Working-class women and men have contributed so much to poetry, both historic and contemporary, much of it in the form of rhyme, ode, and lyrics. Many of these styles of poetry are captured and celebrated in this book. And many recognised poets are rightly given credit for their enduring works.

The poets chosen are recognised for their creative abilities, often exercised in the most appalling of political and personal circumstances.

The poems selected will stir every emotion, from heartbreak to profound love, from pride in bravery to the despair of war. Some poets are well-known, others less so. But all of them are inspiring to read, and their talent is celebrated by Jeremy and Len with words that are personal and passionate.

This book gives the reader an opportunity to look behind the well-documented public profiles of Len and Jeremy to discover the influences that shaped their strong values and beliefs.

What emerges in these pages is an understanding of the strong relationship between the favourite poetry of the two men and their lifetime commitment to progressive politics and activism.

As the Beatles famously sang, 'we get by with a little help from our friends', and this book is no exception. It features contributions from individuals who share a common bond of fighting for fairness, peace, and justice.

Acclaimed actors Maxine Peake and Julie Hesmondhalgh. Iconic film director Ken Loach. Journalist and author Gary Younge. Comedian and writer Francesca Martinez. Author and filmmaker Morag Livingston. Actor, author and comedian Alexei Sayle. Children's author and poet Michael Rosen. Internationally renowned writer and actor Rob Delaney. All have made selections for this book.

Just as socialist and class politics is a collective endeavour, so is poetry that speaks for the many, not the few.

There's a Poet in All of Us

Jeremy Corbyn

The idea for this book grew out of regular conversations Len and I had about poetry: the enjoyment we get from it and the opportunity it provides for escape and inspiration. The hardest part about putting the book together was deciding what to leave out from the countless wonderful poems available.

Poetry tells truths that often cannot be expressed in discourse or prose. It gives meaning to the inner self and allows for people to think freely.

Children frequently write and read poetry in their primary school years. Sadly, when they become teenagers, they often become embarrassed and either retreat into writing in secret or just give up altogether. This book, and the two poetry reading events Len and I appeared at, in Liverpool and at the Edinburgh Festival, were designed to encourage others, and especially young people, to enjoy reading and writing poetry.

Halfway through the evening at the CASA in Liverpool, a young man asked shyly if he could read out his own poem. We of course agreed, and when he did so, he inspired others in the room to do the same. They often read the poems they had written from their phones. It was a wonderful, spontaneous interaction, a public airing of creativity that should always be encouraged. There is a poet in all of us and nobody should ever be afraid of sharing their poetry. It doesn't need to rhyme or scan. It can be just an expression of thoughts that may at first appear as random but, when written down on paper or screen, can become more coherent and take on a deeper meaning.

Poetry Is Food for the Soul

Len McCluskey

I was born in a traditional working-class neighbourhood in Liverpool. We lived in a two-up-two-down terraced house; think of the places in the opening titles of *Coronation Street* and you'll get the picture. Poetry was not on the agenda either at home or at school. Indeed, even when I passed the scholarship and went to Cardinal Godfrey College, poetry played no part in my formal education.

It was the arrival of the musical revolution in the 1960s and the advent of TV bringing the great issues of the day into our living room that led me to start paying attention to the protest songs of the time. The lyrics of those songs captivated me. Along with the artistic revolution taking place in the pubs and clubs in Liverpool, I was suddenly introduced to poetry!

Poetry, to me, is one of the greatest mediums for communication. It expresses the full range of our emotions; it has so much to teach us. I believe it should be compulsory on the National School Curriculum to make it accessible to every student, so that the stigma in working-class communities about poetry only being for 'posh people' or 'softies' would gradually be eliminated. After all, don't we teach our babies and young children nursery rhymes to help them understand and learn? Why shouldn't that apply throughout our school days?

One thing I know is that the beauty of language expressed through rhyme or other forms of verse has given me enormous joy. I always take a poetry book with me on holiday. At home I can often be found in a corner sitting quietly with a poetry book. It's food for the soul. I hope you enjoy my selections and, more importantly, that this book draws you deeper into the world of poetry.

I Wandered Lonely as a Cloud
WILLIAM WORDSWORTH (1770–1850)
Selected by Jeremy

I grew up in rural Wiltshire and have early memories, as a very young child, of flower-covered roadsides and fields. Then, when I was seven years old, we moved to Shropshire, where my childhood exploration of woods and meadows continued and with it a deep appreciation of the natural world and all its wonders.

I recall one of my teachers around that time had a keen appreciation for poetry and read aloud to us traditional, mainly English, poems. My mother enjoyed poetry, too. Though I didn't realise it at the time, these powerful influences were key to developing a love of poetry that endures to this day.

The natural world has always been an inspiration for poets, whose work can not only express its beauty but also teach us about the threats of industrial pollution and the extraction of resources from the earth. Poems about nature can persuade people to live with, not despite, the natural world, in a way that lectures and speeches never can.

William Wordsworth was no radical revolutionary, but by simply describing daffodils in his famous poem 'I Wandered Lonely as a Cloud', he conveys a strong message advocating for environmental sustainability. The second verse is particularly beautiful, but it should be read as part of the whole poem.

∽

I wandered lonely as a cloud
That floats on high o'er vales and hills,
When all at once I saw a crowd,
A host, of golden daffodils;
Beside the lake, beneath the trees,
Fluttering and dancing in the breeze.

Continuous as the stars that shine
And twinkle on the milky way,
They stretched in never-ending line
Along the margin of a bay:
Ten thousand saw I at a glance,
Tossing their heads in sprightly dance.

The waves beside them danced; but they
Out-did the sparkling waves in glee:
A poet could not but be gay,
In such a jocund company:
I gazed—and gazed—but little thought
What wealth the show to me had brought:

For oft, when on my couch I lie
In vacant or in pensive mood,
They flash upon that inward eye
Which is the bliss of solitude;
And then my heart with pleasure fills,
And dances with the daffodils.

If—

RUDYARD KIPLING (1865–1936)

Selected by Len

Rudyard Kipling's 'If—' is frequently voted the nation's favourite poem. I have great affection for it, in part because it makes me think of my dad, who first drew it to my attention and recited it to me when I was a youngster. He felt a special connection to one of the verses and its description of 'pitch-and-toss':

> If you can make one heap of all your winnings
> And risk it on one turn of pitch-and-toss,
> And lose, and start again at your beginnings
> And never breathe a word about your loss

My father told me of his experiences in Belfast's Harland and Wolff shipyard. He was working in Liverpool repairing a ship and followed the vessel to Northern Ireland to finish the job. He recounted the huge gatherings that would assemble on a Sunday in a field near the shipyard, gambling on pitch-and-toss. Big, strong men lashed out with their studded belts to keep the circled crowd in order and prevent anyone encroaching onto the playing area. For me, the story evoked an image of working men trying to escape the drudgery of life while seeking a bit of extra money. And, of course, the consequences for their family when they lost. Gambling, I found out when I was a teenager, is not a good thing when it gets out hand. Fortunately, with a little help from my friends, I was able to sidestep its pitfalls.

The poem's different verses have a specific meaning to many people, hence its popularity. The lines I can especially relate to are certainly applicable to Jeremy as well:

> If you can bear to hear the truth you've spoken
> Twisted by knaves to make a trap for fools,
> [. . .]
> Or being lied about, don't deal in lies,
> Or being hated, don't give way to hating

As for the poet, well, sometimes it's necessary to live with the disappointment of discovering that an artist one loves is less admirable than their work. Take Salvador Dalí for instance. He is one of my favorite painters. I remember being particularly struck by his masterpiece, *Christ of Saint John of the Cross*, that hangs in Scotland's Kelvingrove Museum where it is admired by countless Glaswegians and visitors from all over the world. It was only subsequently that I found out that, though Dalí dallied with the Communist Party in his home country of Spain, he also became friends with the fascist leader General Franco. I've come to accept that one can admire a work of art without feeling the same affection for its creator. For me, that distinction also occurs with Kipling. He was born in India in the days of the Raj and was, from all accounts, a misogynist and racist. His views on Ireland were outrageous. It was a disappointment to discover these facts, but it also led me to learn more about the colonial attitudes created by the British Empire.

If you can keep your head when all about you
    Are losing theirs and blaming it on you,
If you can trust yourself when all men doubt you,
    But make allowance for their doubting too;
If you can wait and not be tired by waiting,
    Or being lied about, don't deal in lies,
Or being hated, don't give way to hating,
    And yet don't look too good, nor talk too wise:

If you can dream—and not make dreams your master;
    If you can think—and not make thoughts your aim;
If you can meet with Triumph and Disaster
    And treat those two impostors just the same;
If you can bear to hear the truth you've spoken
    Twisted by knaves to make a trap for fools,
Or watch the things you gave your life to, broken,
    And stoop and build 'em up with worn-out tools:

If you can make one heap of all your winnings
    And risk it on one turn of pitch-and-toss,
And lose, and start again at your beginnings
    And never breathe a word about your loss;
If you can force your heart and nerve and sinew
    To serve your turn long after they are gone,
And so hold on when there is nothing in you
    Except the Will which says to them: 'Hold on!'

If you can talk with crowds and keep your virtue,
    Or walk with Kings—nor lose the common touch;
If neither foes nor loving friends can hurt you;
    If all men count with you, but none too much;

If you can fill the unforgiving minute
    With sixty seconds' worth of distance run,
Yours is the Earth and everything that's in it,
    And—which is more—you'll be a Man, my son!

Remember

CHRISTINA ROSSETTI (1830–1894)

Selected by Len

The beautiful poem 'Remember' by Christina Rossetti is extremely popular and often read at funerals—I recited it at my mum's. It speaks in a way that touches the depths of your emotions. This is typical of Rossetti's writings and explains why this Victorian woman has, in many ways, outlasted her male contemporaries. She is regarded by many as the foremost female poet of her day. Feminists see her as a symbol of constrained female genius. She was the sister of Dante Gabriel Rossetti, the celebrated artist and poet. Her father was a political exile from Italy and their home was often visited by artists, scholars, and revolutionaries. She was opposed to slavery and animal cruelty. More recently, scholars have explored the deeper meanings of erotic desire and social redemption in her work.

Many of Rossetti's poems have been put to music, including perhaps one of the most famous Christmas carols, 'In the Bleak Midwinter' by Gustav Holst. As well as a romantic poet, she was also a writer of children's verse. 'Goblin Market' is one of her poems that I love to read over and over.

~

Remember me when I am gone away,
    Gone far away into the silent land;
    When you can no more hold me by the hand,
Nor I half turn to go yet turning stay.
Remember me when no more day by day
    You tell me of our future that you plann'd:
    Only remember me; you understand
It will be late to counsel then or pray.
Yet if you should forget me for a while
    And afterwards remember, do not grieve:
    For if the darkness and corruption leave
    A vestige of the thoughts that once I had,
Better by far you should forget and smile
    Than that you should remember and be sad.

The Foggy Dew

CHARLES O'NEILL (1887–1963)

Selected by Len

As a child of the tumultuous '60s in my beloved Liverpool, I couldn't help but become aware of the great causes of the day: the Vietnam War; the Civil Rights movement in America; the anti-apartheid movement in South Africa; and the Catholic Civil Rights movement in Northern Ireland, led by Bernadette Devlin.

Being a Scouser, I always closely followed the developments in Ireland. Liverpool has a deep Irish Catholic community, which likely contributes to the booing of the national anthem by the city's football supporters. But there is a more general antipathy in the city towards the entire English establishment which, on frequent occasions in the '70s, '80s, and '90s, seemed ranged against the people of Liverpool.

Like many in Liverpool, I grew up supporting the cause of a United Ireland. On becoming general secretary of Unite, however, I was careful to respect the different position of our Protestant members in the North. Unite is the largest trade union in the North of Ireland and I preached unity between the two communities on every possible occasion. It was heartening to see workplaces that were predominantly Protestant elect a Catholic shop steward and vice versa. I was delighted by the signing of the Good Friday Agreement.

Nevertheless, the poets of Ireland continued to capture my heart with their romantic portrayals of the 1916 Easter Rising and its Proclamation of Independence from Britain. One of my favourite poems, 'The Foggy Dew', like many Irish and Scottish poems, was put to music. Sinead O'Connor & The Chieftains, The Dubliners, and Shane McGowan of the Pogues have all covered the song.

As down the glen one Easter morn to a
city fair rode I
There armed lines of marching men in
squadrons passed me by
No fife did hum nor battle drum did
sound its dread tattoo
But the Angelus bell o'er the Liffey swell
rang out through the foggy dew

Right proudly high over Dublin town
they hung out the flag of war
'Twas better to die 'neath an Irish sky
than at Suvla or Sedd El Bahr
And from the plains of Royal Meath
strong men came hurrying through
While Britannia's Huns, with their
long-range guns sailed in through the
foggy dew

'Twas England bade our Wild Geese go
that small nations might be free
But their lonely graves are by Suvla's
waves or the shore of the Great North Sea
Oh, had they died by Pearse's side or
fought with Cathal Brugha
Their names we will keep where the

Fenians sleep 'neath the shroud of the foggy dew

But the bravest fell, and the requiem bell rang mournfully and clear
For those who died that Eastertide in the springing of the year
And the world did gaze, in deep amaze, at those fearless men, but few,
Who bore the fight that freedom's light might shine through the foggy dew

Ah, back through the glen I rode again and my heart with grief was sore
For I parted then with valiant men whom I never shall see more
But to and fro in my dreams I go and I'd kneel and pray for you,
For slavery fled, O glorious dead, When you fell in the foggy dew

Let Me Die a Youngman's Death
ROGER McGOUGH (1937–)
Selected by Len

Despite having lived in London for many years, the community in Liverpool means the world to me. The cultural vibrancy of the city is sometimes difficult to explain, but that strong sense of community surely has something to do with it.

The music of Liverpool in the '60s, the so-called Merseybeat, is of course renowned around the world. We Liverpudlians are immensely proud that the Beatles came from our city. The lyrics of Lennon and McCartney will live forever.

Part of the cultural revolution that produced the Mersey sound was the work of the Liverpool poets, notably Roger McGough, Adrian Henri, and Brian Patten. They were working-class lads who went to art college, not university. They read their poetry in pubs and clubs.

S. N. Radhika Lakshmi once said, 'poems should be considered as an agent'—that was the dictum of the Mersey poets too: The effect a poem produces is more important than the poem itself. Their work had 'an undercurrent of sarcasm, irony, and pungent wit'. Their poetry often received a hostile reception from the literary establishment, but Lakshmi likened their style to that of Robert Frost 'with their deft handling of complicated ideas in uncomplicated language.' They paved the way for great artists like John Cooper-Clarke, born in nearby Salford, whose poem 'I Wanna Be Yours' is funny and brilliant.

LET ME DIE A YOUNGMAN'S DEATH

Roger McGough was a member of the group The Scaffold, playing alongside Paul McCartney's brother, Mike, and John Gorman. McGough's poem 'The Leader' has made me smile many times, not least when I was general secretary of Unite.

> I wanna be the leader
> I wanna be the leader
> Can I be the leader?
> Can I? I can?
> Promise? Promise?
> Yippee I'm the leader
> I'm the leader
>
> OK what shall we do?

But the poem by McGough that I have chosen is 'Let Me Die a Youngman's Death', which captures the humour and wit typifying so many of Liverpool's poets.

Let me die a youngman's death
not a clean and inbetween
the sheets holywater death
not a famous-last-words
peaceful out of breath death

When I'm 73
and in constant good tumour
may I be mown down at dawn
by a bright red sports car

on my way home
from an allnight party

Or when I'm 91
with silver hair
and sitting in a barber's chair
may rival gangsters
with hamfisted tommyguns burst in
and give me a short back and insides

Or when I'm 104
and banned from the Cavern
may my mistress
catching me in bed with her daughter
and fearing for her son
cut me up into little pieces
and throw away every piece but one

Let me die a youngman's death
not a free from sin tiptoe in
candle wax and waning death
not a curtains drawn by angels borne
'what a nice way to go' death

The Masque of Anarchy (excerpt)
PERCY BYSSHE SHELLEY (1792–1822)
Selected by Len

In 1819 at Peterloo in Manchester, one of the great acts of establishment oppression took place. Tens of thousands had gathered peacefully to demand a greater say for ordinary people in the nation's government. This gathering is regarded as a significant moment on the path towards democracy. The establishment sent in the cavalry, who charged into the crowd, killing men, women, and children; hundreds were injured. In 2019, on the 200th anniversary of the massacre, director Mike Leigh released his acclaimed film *Peterloo* with my favourite actress, Maxine Peake, in a starring role. I had the privilege of speaking at the launch of the film in London.

When news of the massacre reached Percy Bysshe Shelley in Italy, he was outraged and inspired to write his masterpiece 'The Masque of Anarchy'. He characterises: The ermined gowns as Fraud; Hypocrisy as the bible, church, bishops, lawyers, spies; Anarchy as the King – 'I am God, and King, and Law!'; hired murderers who did sing 'Thou art God, and Law, and King'; but what also emerges - Hope - the people's inherent goodness to rise up against tyranny.

The poem is too long to be reproduced in its entirety here, but I urge readers to take time to absorb the full text, which is as relevant today as it was two hundred years ago. Its final line, 'Ye are many, they are few' has become a clarion call for socialists, not least for the

Labour Party under Jeremy's leadership, which echoed its sentiment in the title for its manifesto. In my view, the last three verses of the poem best evoke the spirit of rebellion on display at Peterloo.

'And that slaughter to the Nation
Shall steam up like inspiration,
Eloquent, oracular;
A volcano heard afar.

'And these words shall then become
Like Oppression's thundered doom,
Ringing through each heart and brain,
Heard again—again—again—

'Rise like Lions after slumber
In unvanquishable number—
Shake your chains to earth like dew
Which in sleep had fall'n on you—
Ye are many—they are few.'

In Jerusalem

MAHMOUD DARWISH (1941–2008)

Selected by Jeremy

Poetry is sometimes the way people under occupation and oppression can best express themselves, often to the confusion of the occupying force. Poetry can be the vehicle for oral history, convey real feelings that need to be disguised, and convey messages of resistance and hope.

I have visited Palestine and Israel on nine occasions and been uplifted and depressed in equal measure by the experiences. On these visits I was made aware of the daily trauma of the occupation. For Palestinians in the West Bank (many of whom have farmed there for generations), having their land seized by settlers and becoming landless and impoverished is part of their new existence.

Jerusalem, with its rich history and teeming life, is a city that always inspires me. But at the same time, it's impossible not to be saddened by the high walls and checkpoints that keep communities apart.

Palestine's best-known poet is Mahmoud Darwish. He published more than thirty books, the first when he was just nineteen years old. He spoke and wrote Hebrew as well as Arabic and French. His first love was a Jewish woman in Haifa, to whom he dedicated poetry. He is a symbol of resistance and the richness of Palestinian culture and history.

Darwish was born in Galilee, Palestine. When Israeli forces arrived in his village, al-Birwa, he and his family fled to Lebanon. The village was razed to the ground. They returned a year later to Israel, where Darwish went to school as a Palestinian in Israel.

Darwish became a member of the Palestinian Communist Party. In 1970 he went to the Soviet Union and studied at Moscow State University. He subsequently moved to Egypt and then Lebanon, where he joined the Palestine Liberation Organisation. He was banned from entering Israel.

His 1974 poem 'In Jerusalem', written seven years after the Six Day War, is a powerful cry against occupation.

In Jerusalem, and I mean within the ancient walls,
I walk from one epoch to another without a memory
to guide me. The prophets over there are sharing
the history of the holy . . . ascending to heaven
and returning less discouraged and melancholy, because love
and peace are holy and are coming to town.
I was walking down a slope and thinking to myself: How
do the narrators disagree over what light said about a stone?
Is it from a dimly lit stone that wars flare up?
I walk in my sleep. I stare in my sleep. I see
no one behind me. I see no one ahead of me.
All this light is for me. I walk. I become lighter. I fly
then I become another. Transfigured. Words
sprout like grass from Isaiah's messenger
mouth: "If you don't believe you won't be safe."
I walk as if I were another. And my wound a white
biblical rose. And my hands like two doves
on the cross hovering and carrying the earth.

I don't walk, I fly, I become another,
transfigured. No place and no time. So who am I?
I am no I in ascension's presence. But I
think to myself: Alone, the prophet Muhammad
spoke classical Arabic. "And then what?"
Then what? A woman soldier shouted:
Is that you again? Didn't I kill you?
I said: You killed me . . . and I forgot, like you, to die.

I Into History, Now (excerpt)
ANDREW SALKEY (1928–1995)
Selected by Jeremy

Andrew Salkey was born in Panama in 1928 but grew up in Jamaica. In 1952, he moved to London to study, write, and teach.

Much of his work was concerned with motivating and educating prominent Black authors of the postwar period about the importance of using history to explain the struggle against colonialism. That struggle brought independence to Ghana in 1957, and most of the Caribbean in the 1960s, with Jamaica achieving it in 1962.

Salkey was acutely aware of the need to include history in the story of modern struggles and did so in his poems and books.

When Salkey's epic poem 'Jamaica' (of which 'I Into History, Now' is the prologue) was published in 1974, it received poor reviews, but it has more than stood the test of time. The poem was quoted during the Windrush debates in Parliament.

Salkey worked on the poem for almost twenty years. He started by making notes only three years after arriving in Britain. He, like many fellow Caribbean people, suffered racism in 1950s London. He had to combine studying, teaching at Tulse Hill School, and working in a theatre as a doorman in order to survive, all the while maintaining his determination to write and encourage others to do so, too.

Salkey was quickly recognised and became a well-known figure in the media. His position as a prominent writer enabled him to develop a whole network of fellow writers in the Caribbean and Africa. He founded, with John La Rose, the Caribbean Artists Movement. Salkey worked with La Rose's Caribbean publishing house and bookshop, New Beacon (which, luckily, is only five minutes' walk from my office in Finsbury Park) as well as Bogle-L'Ouverture Publications, founded by Jessica and Eric Huntley.

He made a massive contribution to the artistic life of the wider Caribbean community and recognised that freeing a country from colonialism takes a lot more than replacing the Union Jack with a new flag: It is about fully recognising the history and culture of slaves and their descendants in the colonies; it is about freeing minds and understanding how empire benefited the wealthy and the traders while suppressing the imagination of the working class.

You see all them
sweet, young fuck walkin'
'cross over so,
over by the drygoods store?

You did know say
that none o' them
know how much history
under them skin,
coil up inside, there so,
like baby hold back from born?

You did know say
that none o' them
or you

know how much them
an' you
an' me
go through,
how, when, how long,
what for
an' where we goin'?

You see all them
rass gal jus' givin'
all o' we cock- stan',
an' movin' easy,
sof', cool breeze,
an' droppin' shadow
where them don't belong?

Is that, yes!

[. . .]

Culture come when you buck up
on you'self.
It start when you' body make shadow
on the lan'
an' you know say
that you standin' up into mirror
underneat' you.

I say to meself,
"Is how the mento music go?"

You say,
"Is how the river flow?"
or, "How the sea does lay down so?"

I done wit' you.
I into history, now.
Is the lan' I want
an' is the lan'
I out to get.

∼

The Negro Speaks of Rivers
LANGSTON HUGHES (1901–1967)
Selected by Jeremy

Langston Hughes, a Black American poet, gave voice and power to Black people facing appalling racism in the twentieth century. One of the early innovators of the literary fusion genre known as jazz poetry, Hughes was a central figure in the Harlem Renaissance. His written work illustrates the delights and difficulties of working-class Black lives with verse that incorporates how Black people talked and the jazz and blues music they played at the time.

In Hughes' own words, his poetry is about 'workers, roustabouts, and singers, and job hunters on Lenox Avenue in New York, or Seventh Street in Washington or South State in Chicago—people up today and down tomorrow, working this week and fired the next, beaten and baffled, but determined not to be wholly beaten, buying furniture on the installment plan, filling the house with roomers to help pay the rent, hoping to get a new suit for Easter—and pawning that suit before the Fourth of July'.

Hughes' work was not without its critics, many of whom deemed his portrayals of Black life to be unattractive and inaccurate. Nevertheless, he became the first Black American to earn a living from his poetry, in part because of his willingness to explore Black identity from a variety of perspectives.

I first heard of Langston Hughes when I lived in Jamaica in the late 1960s and have never forgotten the following lines of his, which featured in an irreverent production for the 1968 Year of Human Rights that we put on at Theatre 77 in Kingston:

DOWN THE LONG HARD ROW THAT I BEEN HOEING
I THOUGHT I HEARD THE HORN OF PLENTY BLOWING

BUT I GOT TO GET A NEW ANTENNA, LORD
MY TV KEEPS ON SNOWING.

I've known rivers:
I've known rivers ancient as the world and older than the
    flow of human blood in human veins.

My soul has grown deep like the rivers.

I bathed in the Euphrates when dawns were young.
I built my hut near the Congo and it lulled me to sleep.
I looked upon the Nile and raised the pyramids above it.
I heard the singing of the Mississippi when Abe Lincoln
        went down to New Orleans, and I've seen
        its muddy bosom turn all golden in the sunset.

I've known rivers:
Ancient, dusky rivers.

My soul has grown deep like the rivers.

Jerusalem
("And did those feet in ancient time")
WILLIAM BLAKE (1757–1827)
Selected by Len

Out of the many ways that one can be drawn to poetry, I remember two instances that led me to engage with the work of William Blake.

The first occurred because of lengthy conversations about Blake that I had with my close friend Mike Carden when we were young shop stewards on the Liverpool docks. Mike was studying for his MA at Warwick University on a one-day-a-week release at the time, and Blake featured heavily in his curriculum. We were both intrigued by the basic tenet of Blakeism: 'Without opposition there is no progress'. I became hooked. My interest was then cemented through one of my favourite films, *Educating Rita*, written by the Liverpool playwright Willy Russell, which features Blake's poetry.

Blake is now regarded as one of the most important poets in history, although during his life he did not receive such acclamation. He was considered by many to be insane, an assessment reinforced by the apparitions he reported seeing, spectres that often inspired his work and underpinned his his metaphysical approach to poetry and engraving. He was a nonconformist who likely met, and was certainly strongly influenced by, Thomas Paine, the great philosopher and author of *The Rights of Man* and *Common Sense*. He also was acquainted with Mary Wollstonecraft, the renowned fighter for women's rights, one of whose books he illustrated. He was a supporter of the French Revolution and the American War of Independence. His most famous poem is perhaps 'The Tyger', but I have chosen 'Jerusalem' for this selection as it seems to me to better reflect his radical beliefs, his writings against the oppressive authority of the Church and State, and his opposition to the Monarchy.

Blake would be astonished, not to say angry, that 'Jerusalem', first published in 1804, has now become a favourite patriotic hymn of the Royal Family and the establishment in general. Blake did not write the poem for the establishment. He was once arrested for sedition after he 'damned the King of England' in an argument with a dragoon. He had educated himself throughout his life and learned Greek, Latin, Hebrew and Italian in order to read scholars in their own languages. He spent his last years in great poverty, and many of his poems described the experiences of being poor. Yet 'Jerusalem' has served as a symbol of British tradition, becoming a staple of the Last Night of the Proms, a patriotic occasion replete with the waving of Union Jacks.

We must remember that 'Jerusalem' was a call to arms, for all nations and working people, and reclaim the poem of a great radical.

And did those feet in ancient time
Walk upon Englands mountains green:
And was the holy Lamb of God,
On Englands pleasant pastures seen!

And did the Countenance Divine,
Shine forth upon our clouded hills?

And was Jerusalem builded here,
Among these dark Satanic Mills?

Bring me my Bow of burning gold:
Bring me my arrows of desire:
Bring me my Spear: O clouds unfold!
Bring me my Chariot of fire!

I will not cease from Mental Fight,
Nor shall my sword sleep in my hand:
Till we have built Jerusalem,
In Englands green & pleasant Land.

The Tree Council

MIKE JENKINS (1953–)

Selected by Jeremy

One of the seminal moments in trade union history is told in the story of the Tolpuddle Martyrs, six agricultural laborers from a village of the same name in Dorset, England, who were arrested for swearing a secret oath, tried, convicted, and transported to Australia. They eventually won the right to return.

My first visit to Tolpuddle was as a child, to see the Martyrs' Cottages and the site where the men swore the oath that led to their arrest. Since then, I have visited Tolpuddle many times for the Martyrs Festival, held every July, a week after the Durham Miner's Gala. It is a key event on the Labour Movement's calendar and features a wonderful march of bands and banners that wind their way through the village and return to rally on the green grass in front of the cottages. The village itself, located just a few miles from Dorchester. is small and well-tended, and surrounded by beautiful countryside.

Many great speeches have been made in Tolpuddle: Michael Foot, then the employment secretary, spoke passionately there in 1974, supporting the Health and Safety at Work Act, which was being blocked in Parliament. Foot pointed out that the big, wealthy agriculture lobby was against the protection of workers and emphasised that farm work was, as it still is, amongst the most dangerous of occupations. Tony Benn's speech on the historical significance of the Martyrs in 2011 had the audience spellbound. And the late Joan Maynard, MP for

Sheffield, spoke in 2021 with brilliance and rage against the tied cottage system for agricultural workers. The festival features music, too. Standout performances for me include Billy Bragg evoking the history of radical, rural England in song, and the Fred Hampton Appreciation Society sharing the music of the Black Panthers.

To this day, the apparent tranquility of rural life often hides a history of poverty, oppression, and suffocating hierarchy that lies just beneath the surface. But such superficial peacefulness was violently interrupted in the early nineteenth century when the galloping pace of the industrial revolution dragged millions from farm work into the big industrial cities. This was a time that saw the rich and powerful flourishing (the wealthy of the City of London spent £20,000—more than two million pounds in today's money—on a banquet to celebrate victory in the Napoleonic wars), but sheer misery for a broad swathe of the population in a widespread economic depression. Former soldiers from the Battle of Waterloo traipsed the country in desperate search for food and work. Rural communities experienced the horror of enclosure, better named as theft, of their common lands whilst landowners reduced wages.

Tolpuddle was no different from thousands of other villages in this period, except for one factor: Six labourers, all God-fearing churchgoers, came together to discuss their opposition to a plan to cut their pay by the owners of the farms where they worked. They decided their common interests required them to stick together, so they formed a union and declared an oath, sworn on the Bible, to support one another.

The response of the landowners was swift and ruthless. The labourers were ostracised, condemned, and charged with sedition and the administration of an illegal oath. They were put on trial at the nearby Dorchester Assize Court in front of a jury composed of their accusers and local landowners. Found guilty, they were sentenced to be taken to Weymouth and placed on a sailing ship that would transport them on the 12,000-mile journey to Australia.

The reaction around the country was powerful. Radical movements across England had been growing since the late seventeenth century. Leigh Hunt, William Godwin, Mary Wollstonecraft, and Percy Shelley, among many others, had been promoting socialist ideas (although they did not call them that at the time). There was a hinterland of thinking, often intertwined with the nonconformist church, that imagined a better world, separate from both feudal landowners and the growing capitalist class in the cities. A campaign in support of the Martyrs grew rapidly, culminating in a huge rally in Copenhagen Fields, a big open space in Islington, just north of St Pancras Church. The campaign was a key factor in the eventual release of the Martyrs and is depicted in a beautiful painting that hangs in Islington Town Hall.

The Martyrs' eventual freedom saw the birth of general trade unionism as an alternative to the more exclusive and protective Guilds for specific skilled trades. The Six, in their bravery, could never have expected what would become of them. They were simply trying to feed their families and be treated with respect.

The Martyr Festival lives on as a reminder of what a small group of people created out of sheer desperation, loyalty to each other, and the determination to make a better world for their children. And Mike Jenkins's poem, 'The Tree Council,' is a great evocation of the time and significance of the events in Tolpuddle.

Under the sycamore's shade
our secret council gathered,
whispers joining the breeze.

We knew gentle blades would fly
just as others spread and grew
in the many places of the desperate.

The canopy enough to hide
our vows and our union,
our shares of the plough.

Six of us sat with promises,
knowing that to bend
was not to break in storms;

knowing that the masters
were experts with their axes;
how easily resolve could be splintered.

There was a future, but no fruit
that we could reach and pick
to feed our needy families.

I spoke up, my brothers agreed,
each plan was a wind
to carry and plant those seeds.

Invictus

WILLIAM ERNEST HENLEY (1849–1903)

Selected by Len

During my youth there was no greater cause than that of the South African anti-apartheid campaign, and as a young shop steward on the Liverpool docks, I was part of that movement. We were involved in all kinds of activities in order to boycott goods and military weapons going to South Africa.

The importance of international solidarity cannot be overstated. I have been involved in many such campaigns over my lifetime:

- The Chile Solidarity Campaign, which swung into action when the democratically elected President Salvador Allende was overthrown by a CIA-backed military coup. Tens of thousands were tortured, murdered, or simply disappeared (for more on these events, see the great 1982 film *Missing*, starring Jack Lemmon and Sissy Spacek). The perpetrator of this evil, General Pinochet, was admired and befriended by Margaret Thatcher.
- The Cuba Solidarity Campaign, which sought to end the U.S. blockade of that beautiful country (a blockade is illegal under UN international law).
- The continued fight for justice for the Palestinian people and the end of the illegal occupation of settlements by the Israeli government.

- The movement in opposition to the sale of arms to Saudi Arabia, which is using British-made weapons to slaughter the Yemeni people.

We must resist these atrocities. International solidarity means so much to people who are being oppressed. Feeling supported by millions around the world can be an enormous encouragement to those on the frontline.

Think of Nelson Mandela: a courageous man who became the symbol of dignified resistance to the state and inspired millions to challenge the evil of apartheid. Not everyone was supportive: Margaret Thatcher called Mandela a terrorist, which says much about her own creed. But had there been an election for world president, Mandela would have won by a landslide. Instead, he was imprisoned from 1964 to 1982 on Robben Island, off the coast of Cape Town, for his anti-apartheid work.

In 1988, rock stars performed at Wembley to celebrate his seventieth birthday, with the songs 'Mandela Day' by Simple Minds and 'Nelson Mandela' by The Specials. These songs echoed around the world, reaching an audience of 600 million in sixty-seven countries. The event's popularity is thought to have increased pressure on the South African government to release Mandela, which they eventually did, although it took an additional twenty months.

It was at Robben Island that Mandela memorised and regularly recited the poem 'Invictus', written by William Ernest Henley in 1875. It was his favourite poem.

Out of the night that covers me,
    Black as the pit from pole to pole,
I thank whatever gods may be
    For my unconquerable soul.

In the fell clutch of circumstance
    I have not winced nor cried aloud.
Under the bludgeonings of chance
    My head is bloody, but unbowed.

Beyond this place of wrath and tears
    Looms but the Horror of the shade,
And yet the menace of the years
    Finds, and shall find me unafraid.

It matters not how strait the gate,
    How charged with punishments the scroll,
I am the master of my fate,
    I am the captain of my soul.

The Schoolboy

WILLIAM BLAKE (1757–1827)

Selected by Jeremy

William Blake, the great mystic, is, as Len has already pointed out, most famous for his poem 'Jerusalem', which was set to music by Hubert Parry during the First World War, more than a century after Blake wrote it. It has become a canonical song with a different appeal to different tastes. It provides a narrative of hope in the darkest of times.

Blake was frequently stressed, usually poor, and almost always misunderstood. Born in Soho in 1757, he left London just once, spending three years in Sussex where he was tried and acquitted for sedition when he allegedly assaulted a soldier and declared, 'Damn the king!' He worked as an engraver and illustrator, living through one of the most tumultuous times in history, the French Revolution, which challenged the notion of eternal monarchic power. The consequent war between Britain and France led to a profound oppression of free speech and the silencing of any dissent.

Following Blake's death in 1827, his devoted wife, Catherine, together with his friends, took up the distribution and sale of his remaining work, but not before his executors went through his writings and burnt many plays, deeming their content to be too sexual and erotic for future generations. However, a vast array of poems and prose survived, including the well-known *Songs of Innocence and of Experience*, originally published in 1789.

I have chosen a short poem from that collection, 'The Schoolboy'. In describing the sorrow of a boy going to school on a summer morning, Blake observed our removal from nature and simultaneous dependence on it as the fast-growing industrial London ate up his beloved fields and brooks throughout Islington and Camden.

The poem yearns for space, freedom, and imagination, and includes the poignant line:

> How can the bird that born for joy
> Sit in a cage and sing.

I love to rise in a summer morn,
When the birds sing on every tree;
The distant huntsman winds his horn,
And the sky-lark sings with me.
O! what sweet company.

But to go to school in a summer morn,
O! it drives all joy away;
Under a cruel eye outworn.
The little ones spend the day,
In sighing and dismay.

Ah! then at times I drooping sit,
And spend many an anxious hour.
Nor in my book can I take delight,
Nor sit in learning's bower,
Worn thro' with the dreary shower.

How can the bird that is born for joy,
Sit in a cage and sing.
How can a child when fears annoy,
But droop his tender wing,
And forget his youthful spring.

O! father & mother, if buds are nip'd,
And blossoms blown away,
And if the tender plants are strip'd
Of their joy in the springing day,
By sorrow and care's dismay.

How shall the summer arise in joy,
Or the summer fruits appear.
Or how shall we gather what griefs destroy
Or bless the mellowing year,
When the blasts of winter appear.

The Lark Ascending

GEORGE MEREDITH (1828–1909)

Selected by Jeremy

Poems on the environment can often be edgy and poignant. Take, for instance, the work of John Clare. He was a farm worker who, suffering from deep depression, spent time in a mental health institution in Northampton. He wrote poetry that captured his anguish at the irreversible changes to the countryside that came about with land enclosures and the industrialisation of agriculture in the nineteenth century. In four lines from 'Elegy on the Ruins of Pickworth', Clare describes the loss of a dilapidated stately home and its replacement with a farm worker's cottage whose occupants could barely survive. At one level he is pining for the old, feudal order but, at another, he is describing the pain that the industrial revolution wrought on rural as well as urban communities.

> And here while Grandeur, with unequal share,
>   Perhaps maintain'd its idleness and pride,
> Industry's cottage rose contented there,
>   With scarce so much as wants of life supplied.

Poets are often closely connected to nature, and frequently draw inspiration from it. The lark, with its beautiful song, appears with notable regularity in poetry and music alike. Len, as an avid Liverpool FC fan (well, nobody's perfect), would likely draw attention to its appearance in 'You'll Never Walk Alone', originally written by Rogers and Hammerstein for their musical *Carousel*.

George Meredith, born in 1828, wrote 'The Lark Ascending' during the later part of his life, in 1881. He was by then an established and revered novelist, one of the most prominent authors of his day. Meredith's description of the lark is so beautiful that it inspired the English composer Ralph Vaughan Williams to write music for it. Williams composed the accompaniment while holidaying in Margate on the day the First World War broke out.

Hearing Vaughan Williams' rendition of 'The Lark Ascending' on the violin gives me goosebumps. I always associate the piece with the First World War, which Meredith never saw.

∼

He rises and begins to round,
He drops the silver chain of sound
Of many links without a break,
In chirrup, whistle, slur and shake,
All intervolv'd and spreading wide,
Like water-dimples down a tide
Where ripple ripple overcurls
And eddy into eddy whirls;
A press of hurried notes that run
So fleet they scarce are more than one,
Yet changingly the trills repeat
And linger ringing while they fleet,
Sweet to the quick o' the ear, and dear
To her beyond the handmaid ear,
Who sits beside our inner springs,
Too often dry for this he brings,

Which seems the very jet of earth
At sight of sun, her music's mirth,
As up he wings the spiral stair,
A song of light, and pierces air
With fountain ardor, fountain play,
To reach the shining tops of day,
And drink in everything discern'd
An ecstasy to music turn'd,
Impell'd by what his happy bill
Disperses; drinking, showering still,
Unthinking save that he may give
His voice the outlet, there to live
Renew'd in endless notes of glee,
So thirsty of his voice is he,
For all to hear and all to know
That he is joy, awake, aglow,
The tumult of the heart to hear
Through pureness filter'd crystal-clear,
And know the pleasure sprinkled bright
By simple singing of delight,
Shrill, irreflective, unrestrain'd,
Rapt, ringing, on the jet sustain'd
Without a break, without a fall,
Sweet-silvery, sheer lyrical,
Perennial, quavering up the chord
Like myriad dews of sunny sward
That trembling into fulness shine,
And sparkle dropping argentine;
Such wooing as the ear receives
From zephyr caught in choric leaves
Of aspens when their chattering net
Is flush'd to white with shivers wet;

And such the water-spirit's chime
On mountain heights in morning's prime,
Too freshly sweet to seem excess,
Too animate to need a stress;
But wider over many heads
The starry voice ascending spreads,
Awakening, as it waxes thin,
The best in us to him akin;
And every face to watch him rais'd,
Puts on the light of children prais'd,
So rich our human pleasure ripes
When sweetness on sincereness pipes,
Though nought be promis'd from the seas,
But only a soft-ruffling breeze
Sweep glittering on a still content,
Serenity in ravishment.

For singing till his heaven fills,
'T is love of earth that he instils,
And ever winging up and up,
Our valley is his golden cup,
And he the wine which overflows
To lift us with him as he goes:
The woods and brooks, the sheep and kine
He is, the hills, the human line,
The meadows green, the fallows brown,
The dreams of labor in the town;
He sings the sap, the quicken'd veins;
The wedding song of sun and rains
He is, the dance of children, thanks
Of sowers, shout of primrose-banks,
And eye of violets while they breathe;

All these the circling song will wreathe,
And you shall hear the herb and tree,
The better heart of men shall see,
Shall feel celestially, as long
As you crave nothing save the song.
Was never voice of ours could say
Our inmost in the sweetest way,
Like yonder voice aloft, and link
All hearers in the song they drink:
Our wisdom speaks from failing blood,
Our passion is too full in flood,
We want the key of his wild note
Of truthful in a tuneful throat,
The song seraphically free
Of taint of personality,
So pure that it salutes the suns
The voice of one for millions,
In whom the millions rejoice
For giving their one spirit voice.

Yet men have we, whom we revere,
Now names, and men still housing here,
Whose lives, by many a battle-dint
Defaced, and grinding wheels on flint,
Yield substance, though they sing not, sweet
For song our highest heaven to greet:
Whom heavenly singing gives us new,
Enspheres them brilliant in our blue,
From firmest base to farthest leap,
Because their love of Earth is deep,
And they are warriors in accord
With life to serve and pass reward,

So touching purest and so heard
In the brain's reflex of yon bird;
Wherefore their soul in me, or mine,
Through self-forgetfulness divine,
In them, that song aloft maintains,
To fill the sky and thrill the plains
With showerings drawn from human stores,
As he to silence nearer soars,
Extends the world at wings and dome,
More spacious making more our home,
Till lost on his aërial rings
In light, and then the fancy sings.

Do not go gentle into that good night

DYLAN THOMAS (1914–1953)

Selected by Len

The city of Liverpool has strong Gaelic links. During the great famines of the 1800s, Irish immigrants travelled via Liverpool, planning to emigrate from there to the U.S. But thousands ended up staying in the city, or instead moved on to London or Glasgow. Lesser known is the fact that in addition to the wave of Irish immigration, a significant number of Welsh people also arrived in Liverpool at this time, including many thousands of building workers. In Walton, an area of Liverpool where my mum and dad lived, there is a row of terraced streets whose first letters spell out the first names of two builders, Owen Elias and his son, William: **O**xton, **W**inslow, **E**ton, and **N**eston; and **W**ilburn, **I**smay, Lind, Lowell, Index, Arnot, and Monty.

Much of my misspent youth took place in North Wales, in the holiday camps of Prestatyn, Rhyl, and Towyn. I feel a strong affinity for Wales, and I love the lilt of the Welsh language.

There have been many great Welsh orators over the decades, none more so than Dylan Thomas, a pacifist and anti-fascist who sympathised with the radical Left. He was known for his radio broadcasts. And while his poems and writings were also popular during his lifetime, his alcoholism ensured that he was doomed as a career poet. He suffered from bronchitis and asthma as well and died in New York in 1953 at the age of just thirty-nine.

Welsh actor Richard Burton read Thomas's play, 'Under Milk Wood', on the radio, and when I heard it, it blew me away. Burton's voice is, of course, wonderful, but Thomas's words were magical. I have to confess: The only way I can read 'Under Milk Wood' is alone, out loud, with a Welsh accent.

The Thomas poem I've chosen for this book, published in 1951, is often read at funerals. I'm trying to persuade my eldest son, Ian, to recite it when my time comes. But at the event at the CASA where the seed of the idea for this book was germinated, I pointed out that the poem has an important message for Jeremy too, one I am pleased to say he seems to have taken to heart.

Do not go gentle into that good night,
Old age should burn and rave at close of day;
Rage, rage against the dying of the light.

Though wise men at their end know dark is right,
Because their words had forked no lightning they
Do not go gentle into that good night.

Good men, the last wave by, crying how bright
Their frail deeds might have danced in a green bay,
Rage, rage against the dying of the light.

Wild men who caught and sang the sun in flight,
And learn, too late, they grieved it on its way,
Do not go gentle into that good night.

Grave men, near death, who see with blinding sight
Blind eyes could blaze like meteors and be gay,
Rage, rage against the dying of the light.

And you, my father, there on the sad height,
Curse, bless, me now with your fierce tears, I pray.
Do not go gentle into that good night.
Rage, rage against the dying of the light.

A Far Cry from Africa
DEREK WALCOTT (1930–2017)
Selected by Jeremy

The Caribbean poets of the post–World War II period wrote about the beauty of the islands and their lives there, the shock of migrating as part of the Windrush generation, and the racism they faced on arrival in Britain. Their poetry was deeply political, capturing the visions of Marcus Garvey's Pan-Africanist campaign and the Rastafari movement, both of which sought to reject European and British colonial culture and reclaim African unity and heritage.

My best education was in Jamaica, where I lived as a volunteer teacher in the 1960s. Looking back, I learned far more than I was able to teach. Jamaica at that time was newly independent, cultivating a national identity through poetry and music that reached back to Africa, where the vast majority of Jamaican ancestors had been captured during the evils of the slave trade. I was deeply influenced by the bravery and imagination of the Caribbean writers and poets who successfully developed a Caribbean literary identity, bringing together the history of the islands and the African slave past of so many of the people.

Poet and playwright Derek Walcott was born in 1930 in Saint Lucia, a former British colony in the West Indies. He divided his life between Saint Lucia, New York, and Boston before he passed away in 2017. His poem 'A Far Cry from Africa', published in 1962, explores the history of the Mau Mau uprising in Kenya, when the Kikuyu people fought for independence from British colonial rule.

A wind is ruffling the tawny pelt
Of Africa. Kikuyu, quick as flies,
Batten upon the bloodstreams of the veldt.
Corpses are scattered through a paradise.
Only the worm, colonel of carrion, cries:
"Waste no compassion on these separate dead!"
Statistics justify and scholars seize
The salients of colonial policy.
What is that to the white child hacked in bed?
To savages, expendable as Jews?

Threshed out by beaters, the long rushes break
In a white dust of ibises whose cries
Have wheeled since civilization's dawn
From the parched river or beast-teeming plain.
The violence of beast on beast is read
As natural law, but upright man
Seeks his divinity by inflicting pain.
Delirious as these worried beasts, his wars
Dance to the tightened carcass of a drum,
While he calls courage still that native dread
Of the white peace contracted by the dead.

Again brutish necessity wipes its hands
Upon the napkin of a dirty cause, again
A waste of our compassion, as with Spain,
The gorilla wrestles with the superman.

I who am poisoned with the blood of both,
Where shall I turn, divided to the vein?
I who have cursed
The drunken officer of British rule, how choose
Between this Africa and the English tongue I love?
Betray them both, or give back what they give?
How can I face such slaughter and be cool?
How can I turn from Africa and live?

Sonnet to Liberty

OSCAR WILDE (1854–1900)

Selected by Len

I am a big fan of Oscar Wilde. The incredible genius of the man is evident in all his plays and the only novel he wrote, *The Picture of Dorian Gray*. His witticisms are intensely memorable. Here are a couple I particularly enjoy:

> I can resist anything but temptation.
> Whenever I get the urge to exercise, I lie down until the feeling passes.

And my absolute favourite, which could apply to both Jeremy and me (each of us known for our lack of punctuality):

> Punctuality is the thief of time.

Wilde wrote forty-three poems. His most famous, 'The Ballad of Reading Gaol' (which is too long to be reproduced for this book), was written after he served two years' hard labour in prison for 'gross indecency'. Wilde had launched a libel case against the Marquess of Queensbury, the aristocrat father of Lord Alfred Douglass, a younger man with whom Wilde had a relationship. It was at this famous trial that the immortal phrase 'a love that dare not speak its name' was first coined, as a euphemism for homosexuality. Wilde's poem tells, with deep emotion, the story of the weeks leading up to the hanging of one of his fellow inmates.

Wilde's time spent in gaol badly damaged his health and ultimately led to his death in Paris in 1900. He was buried in Père Lachaise Cemetery. Incidentally, this is an extraordinary cemetery and well worth a visit. Jim Morrison, lead singer of The Doors, is also buried there.

It's sad and scandalous to think of how many gay people have suffered the pain and fear of criminality and humiliation because of their sexuality. The law that made homosexuality a crime in England was only abolished in 1967. No person, regardless of their gender identity or sexuality, should ever be discriminated against.

I am reminded of the case of Alan Turing who was responsible for breaking the Enigma code during the Second World War that led to the defeat of Nazi Germany. Historians have calculated that this breakthrough saved the lives of 14 million people (there is a wonderful film, *The Imitation Game*, that tells the story). He was a genius, but in 1952 he was convicted of homosexuality and to avoid going to prison he was chemically castrated. He committed suicide two years later in 1954.

In 2009 the Prime Minister, Gordon Brown, made a public apology for Turing's appalling treatment and the Queen later granted a posthumous pardon. In 2019 he was voted by a BBC audience as the Greatest British Person of the 20th Century. His face features on the current £50 note.

∼

Not that I love thy children, whose dull eyes
See nothing save their own unlovely woe,
Whose minds know nothing, nothing care to know,—
But that the roar of thy Democracies,

SONNET TO LIBERTY

Thy reigns of Terror, thy great Anarchies,
Mirror my wildest passions like the sea,—
And give my rage a brother——! Liberty!
For this sake only do thy dissonant cries
Delight my discreet soul, else might all kings
By bloody knout or treacherous cannonades
Rob nations of their rights inviolate
And I remain unmoved—and yet, and yet,
These Christs that die upon the barricades,
God knows it I am with them, in some things.

You Foolish Men

SOR JUANA INÉS DE LA CRUZ (1651–1695)

Selected by Jeremy

In my poetry selections for this book I have tried to provide a broad range of poets and their experiences from all over the globe. Poets writing in the most desperate of times are a constant source of inspiration and help my own understanding of history.

'You Foolish Men' by Sor Juana Inés de la Cruz is a poem hardly known in Europe or North America but is much better known in Mexico. Born in the middle of the seventeenth century, Sor Juana grew up mostly on her grandfather's hacienda in Amecameca, in the state of Morellos, Mexico. The area is home to the oldest olive tree in the Americas and the chapel where Sor Juana lived, under the watchful gaze of the El Popo snowcapped volcano.

Laura and I have visited the Hacienda Panoaya; indeed, we were married there in 2012. Sor Juana and Mary Wollstonecraft's writings were on our wedding invitations.

Sor Juana, the illegitimate daughter of a Spanish colonial officer and an Aztec woman, was a brilliant child. All contemporary accounts of her life speak of how she taught herself Latin and Spanish, in addition to her native Nahuatl. She wrote extensively on the rights of women more than a hundred years before Wollstonecraft would publish the far better known *A Vindication on the Rights of Women*. Sor Juana's formidable intellect came alive in her writing.

After entering a convent, she held salons for well-connected women in Mexico to discuss the way women were treated and prevented from accessing formal education. But as time went on, the group was seen as a threat to the patriarchs of the Catholic Church, who held absolute colonial power at that time. Catholic teachings were destroying the Aztec and Mayan civilisations, suppressing their languages and imposing Latin and Spanish instead. Although Sor Juana had some support from those in the Church who recognised her brilliance, paranoia took over and she was ordered to cease her intellectual work and writing. She was told a woman's place was not teaching or learning, and she was forced out of the Church. She died in 1695, still in her mid-forties, from a fever contracted while comforting impoverished people suffering from the plague.

Most of Sor Juana's work has been lost or destroyed, but Mexican poet Octavio Paz has translated the writing that survived and written extensively about her life to help give her the recognition she deserves. After almost three hundred years, the state of Mexico finally recognised her contribution to the country's cultural heritage. We can only imagine what powerful work she might have produced had she lived longer, but what we can read is both witty and inspirational: 'You Foolish Men', devastating in its critique of arrogant men and their hypocrisy, is as apposite today as it was in the late seventeenth century.

You foolish men who lay
the guilt on women,
not seeing you're the cause
of the very thing you blame;

if you invite their disdain
with measureless desire
why wish they well behave
if you incite to ill.

You fight their stubbornness,
then, weightily,
you say it was their lightness
when it was your guile.

In all your crazy shows
you act just like a child
who plays the bogeyman
of which he's then afraid.

With foolish arrogance
you hope to find a Thais
in her you court, but a Lucretia
when you've possessed her.

What kind of mind is odder
than his who mists
a mirror and then complains
that it's not clear.

Their favour and disdain
you hold in equal state,
if they mistreat, you complain,
you mock if they treat you well.

No woman wins esteem of you:
the most modest is ungrateful

if she refuses to admit you;
yet if she does, she's loose.

You always are so foolish
your censure is unfair;
one you blame for cruelty
the other for being easy.

What must be her temper
who offends when she's
ungrateful and wearies
when compliant?

But with the anger and the grief
that your pleasure tells
good luck to her who doesn't love you
and you go on and complain.

Your lover's moans give wings
to women's liberty:
and having made them bad,
you want to find them good.

Who has embraced
the greater blame in passion?
She who, solicited, falls,
or he who, fallen, pleads?

Who is more to blame,
though either should do wrong?
She who sins for pay
or he who pays to sin?

Why be outraged at the guilt
that is of your own doing?
Have them as you make them
or make them what you will.

Leave off your wooing
and then, with greater cause,
you can blame the passion
of her who comes to court?

Patent is your arrogance
that fights with many weapons
since in promise and insistence
you join world, flesh and devil.

"Hope" is the thing with feathers
EMILY DICKINSON (1830–1886)

The Road Not Taken
ROBERT FROST (1874–1963)

Selected by Len

The protest songs of the '60s struck a chord in me that has guided my life. Their lyrics were poetry put to music and told a profound message. Bob Dylan's song 'Blowing in the Wind' was a wake-up call as well as a call to arms.

Paul Simon is an amazing and alluring wordsmith. During the Vietnam War, he wrote a lesser-known song, 'On the Side of a Hill', which told the story of a young seven-year-old boy killed in the war, and how a little cloud drops tears on his grave. This verse lives with me 50 years later:

> And generals order their men to kill
> And to fight for a cause long ago forgotten
> While a little cloud weeps on the side of a hill

The beauty of Simon's lyricism has opened doors to other poets for me. In his song 'The Dangling Conversation' he speaks of Emily Dickinson and Robert Frost. Here are my favourite poems from each:

'"Hope" is the thing with feathers', published by Emily Dickinson in 1891. This poem is so beautifully written and speaks to all of us about the greatest emotion, hope, and how fragile it can be.

'The Road Not Taken', published by Robert Frost in 1916. This poem is so relevant to my life, it makes me think back on how many times I have chosen a path to follow, only to wonder what my life would have been like had I chosen another direction.

"Hope" is the thing with feathers
EMILY DICKINSON

"Hope" is the thing with feathers -
That perches in the soul -
And sings the tune without the words -
And never stops - at all -

And sweetest - in the Gale - is heard -
And sore must be the storm -
That could abash the little Bird
That kept so many warm -

I've heard it in the chillest land -
And on the strangest Sea -
Yet - never - in Extremity,
It asked a crumb - of me.

The Road Not Taken
ROBERT FROST

Two roads diverged in a yellow wood,
And sorry I could not travel both
And be one traveler, long I stood
And looked down one as far as I could
To where it bent in the undergrowth;

Then took the other, as just as fair,
And having perhaps the better claim,
Because it was grassy and wanted wear;
Though as for that the passing there
Had worn them really about the same,

And both that morning equally lay
In leaves no step had trodden black.
Oh, I kept the first for another day!
Yet knowing how way leads on to way,
I doubted if I should ever come back.

I shall be telling this with a sigh
Somewhere ages and ages hence:
Two roads diverged in a wood, and I—
I took the one less traveled by,
And that has made all the difference.

Dulce et Decorum Est

WILFRED OWEN (1893–1918)

Selected by Len

Campaigns for peace and justice have always been important in my life, particularly efforts that resist the devastation that war brings.

The horrors of any conflict are now brought via TV or the internet directly into our living rooms, but in the past we had to rely on war correspondents and historians to share the reality of the horrific scenes playing out on the battlefield.

Poets of both the past and present help to drive home these brutal experiences of war. There have been so many powerful war poems written throughout history. The poetry of World War I includes poems that are jingoistic and glorifying the fight for King and Country but also poems that are virulently anti-war. British poet Wilfred Owen's work falls into the latter category, and my favourite poem of his, surely among the best ever written, is 'Dulce et Decorum Est', published in 1920.

Many World War I poets fought in the front line and witnessed first-hand the hopeless devastation of human life. Owen was killed in 1918, aged just twenty-five—a week before Armistice. What a tragic loss of a genius at such a young age, like the millions of young people whose lives have been wasted by an uncaring and dismissive establishment.

The English translation of the poem's Latin title is: 'It is sweet and proper to die for one's country'. These words are engraved on the wall in Sandhurst Military Academy. That's why Owen called it 'the old lie'.

Bent double, like old beggars under sacks,
Knock-kneed, coughing like hags, we cursed through sludge,
Till on the haunting flares we turned our backs,
And towards our distant rest began to trudge.
Men marched asleep. Many had lost their boots
But limped on, blood-shod. All went lame; all blind;
Drunk with fatigue; deaf even to the hoots
Of gas-shells dropping softly behind.

Gas! GAS! Quick, boys!—An ecstasy of fumbling
Fitting the clumsy helmets just in time,
But someone still was yelling out and stumbling
And flound'ring like a man in fire or lime.—
Dim through the misty panes and thick green light,
As under a green sea, I saw him drowning.

In all my dreams before my helpless sight,
He plunges at me, guttering, choking, drowning.

If in some smothering dreams, you too could pace
Behind the wagon that we flung him in,
And watch the white eyes writhing in his face,
His hanging face, like a devil's sick of sin;
If you could hear, at every jolt, the blood
Come gargling from the froth-corrupted lungs,

Obscene as cancer, bitter as the cud
Of vile, incurable sores on innocent tongues,—
My friend, you would not tell with such high zest
To children ardent for some desperate glory,
The old Lie: *Dulce et decorum est*
Pro patria mori.

Dead Man's Dump

ISAAC ROSENBERG (1890–1918)

Selected by Jeremy

Poetry is sometimes so powerful it can inspire people in the most appalling of circumstances to fight for political change.

One of the most creative uses of poetry during a time of adversity was World War I, when millions of young men from all over Europe and the European colonies poured onto the Western Front to die fighting the first industrial war. So many died in those trenches, at such young ages. We can only imagine the greatness they would have achieved had they survived.

The best-known war poets of this period were Siegfried Sassoon, Rupert Brooke, and Wilfred Owen, who wrote of the feelings of fear and despair buried within the trenches, waiting for the call to climb over the top and rush into battle.

There are poets on all sides in every war who question the danger and certain death they are facing, and wonder: Why? For what? Wars produce poetry that eludes any traditional historical analysis, for it tells truths in a deeply emergent, personal way.

Isaac Rosenberg, a young Jewish man born in 1890 who grew up in the east of London, volunteered to be a soldier so he could use his pay to support his impoverished mother. He was killed at the Somme in 1918.

I learned about Rosenberg's short and fascinating life through two wonderful and warm books by Chris Searle (famous for *Stepney Words*, an anthology of poems by the pupils at the school where he taught, and a lifetime spent fighting racism). *Isaac and I* (2017) details how much of Searle's own life and ideas about justice and peace were inspired by Rosenberg's poetry, and *Whitechapel Boy*, published a year later, chronicles Rosenberg's life, the pleasures and poverty of life in Whitechapel at the turn of the century, and the descent into the horrors of the First World War.

Rosenberg's most powerful poem, in my opinion, is 'Dead Man's Dump'. The last verse is both horrific and extraordinary in describing how bodies are taken from the war front to communal burial places.

The plunging limbers over the shattered track
Racketed with their rusty freight,
Stuck out like many crowns of thorns,
And the rusty stakes like sceptres old
To stay the flood of brutish men
Upon our brothers dear.

The wheels lurched over sprawled dead
But pained them not, though their bones crunched,
Their shut mouths made no moan.
They lie there huddled, friend and foeman,
Man born of man, and born of woman,
And shells go crying over them
From night till night and now.

Earth has waited for them,
All the time of their growth
Fretting for their decay:
Now she has them at last!
In the strength of their strength
Suspended—stopped and held.

What fierce imaginings their dark souls lit?
Earth! have they gone into you!
Somewhere they must have gone,
And flung on your hard back
Is their soul's sack
Emptied of God-ancestralled essences.
Who hurled them out? Who hurled?

None saw their spirits' shadow shake the grass,
Or stood aside for the half used life to pass
Out of those doomed nostrils and the doomed mouth,
When the swift iron burning bee
Drained the wild honey of their youth.

What of us who, flung on the shrieking pyre,
Walk, our usual thoughts untouched,
Our lucky limbs as on ichor fed,
Immortal seeming ever?
Perhaps when the flames beat loud on us,
A fear may choke in our veins
And the startled blood may stop.

The air is loud with death,
The dark air spurts with fire,
The explosions ceaseless are.

Timelessly now, some minutes past,
Those dead strode time with vigorous life,
Till the shrapnel called 'An end!'
But not to all. In bleeding pangs
Some borne on stretchers dreamed of home,
Dear things, war-blotted from their hearts.

Maniac Earth! howling and flying, your bowel
Seared by the jagged fire, the iron love,
The impetuous storm of savage love.
Dark Earth! dark Heavens! swinging in chemic smoke,
What dead are born when you kiss each soundless soul
With lightning and thunder from your mined heart,
Which man's self dug, and his blind fingers loosed?

A man's brains splattered on
A stretcher-bearer's face;
His shook shoulders slipped their load,
But when they bent to look again
The drowning soul was sunk too deep
For human tenderness.

They left this dead with the older dead,
Stretched at the cross roads.

Burnt black by strange decay
Their sinister faces lie,
The lid over each eye,
The grass and coloured clay
More motion have than they,
Joined to the great sunk silences.

Here is one not long dead;
His dark hearing caught our far wheels,
And the choked soul stretched weak hands
To reach the living word the far wheels said,
The blood-dazed intelligence beating for light,
Crying through the suspense of the far torturing wheels
Swift for the end to break
Or the wheels to break,
Cried as the tide of the world broke over his sight.

Will they come? Will they ever come?
Even as the mixed hoofs of the mules,
The quivering-bellied mules,
And the rushing wheels all mixed
With his tortured upturned sight.
So we crashed round the bend,
We heard his weak scream,
We heard his very last sound,
And our wheels grazed his dead face.

Ballad of a Bushman

WENDELL BROWN (1945–2014)

Selected by Jeremy

Whilst looking for appropriate readings for our Liverpool Poetry evening in 2021, I found a wonderful poem: 'Ballad of a Bushman'.

The writer, Wendell Brown, first read it in West Los Angeles in 2013. Like many veterans of the Vietnam War, Brown was drafted to serve in 1967. It was just after his daughter was born. He served in the U.S. army in Qui Nhon, in the Bin Dinh province of Vietnam. One day, he was being pursued by the Viet Cong, and a young woman offered him a safe hiding place in a village hut. His pursuers arrived and stabbed her to death. Brown lost control and fired repeatedly, killing two soldiers and an officer of the Viet Cong. These events scarred him deeply, and he suffered visions and nightmares for the rest of his life.

In 1983, while working as a bricklayer, he experienced a flashback of the woman's death that caused him to fall from scaffolding and dislocate his back. Struggling with the emotional and physical fall-out from his injury, as well as other psychological trauma from the Vietnam War, Brown was unable to work, and resorted to living on the streets of Brentwood, Los Angeles. He read poetry for small amounts of money, and this is where 'Ballad of a Bushman' comes from.

Brown was one of tens of thousands of African Americans whose lives were permanently damaged by the military and war. Wars never end in the minds of those who serve. In the U.S., more Vietnam-era soldiers have died from suicide than were killed in conflict.

Brown died in 2014 and was buried at the Arkansas State Veterans cemetery in Little Rock. 'Ballad of a Bushman' is his story and his dream.

Some clustered bushes shelter me,
In loneliness and misery,
They shield me from the wind and cold,
And help keep back what hopes I hold.

I gave my best for Uncle Sam,
And came back dead from Viet Nam,
When afterwards at home again,
Just one among forgotten men.

My world had changed, I was alone.
Nobody cared. No welcome shown.
From eyes of stranger, eyes of friends
My heart was broken, would not mend.

Such awful scenes of dead mankind
Blood-soaked the regions of my mind.
For me the loss of days, long gone,
Leave me no choice, but to wander on.

What do I seek and do not find?
Where is the comfort for my kind?
No cheerful hearth awaits for me.
My days plod on eternally.

But wait I say don't pity me.
I have the mountains and the sea.
I've watched the cities sprawl and grow,
With "people-boxes" row on row.

I've seen men slaving lives away.
Pursuing money night and day,
Confined in concrete kennels high,
Commercial treadmills in the sky.

I too need money, that is true.
In meager bits I beg from you.
I am not proud, I have no wealth.
I am thankful just to have my health.

My wants are few, but this I've found,
What peace is mine, comes from the ground.
God's friendly bushes are my "pad"
They gave what little ease I've had.

They know full well I sometimes cry.
They know, as I, that men must die.
Before that time I want life
With simple comforts, kids and wife.

For now, I live the life I've got.
A victim of the war I fought.
The bushes know, I'm sure they do
They shelter me, and others too.

They always greet me as a man.
They keep me warm as best they can.

They shade me from the blazing sun.
And welcome me when the day is done.

But how long will my bushes stand
As urban growth spreads across the land?
I pray for bushes. Let them be.
They make a "home" for now, for me.

For Whom the Bell Tolls

JOHN DONNE (1572–1631)

Selected by Len

I discovered this next poem through none other than Ernest Hemingway. Hemingway lived an adventurous and admirable life. He knew many of the famous artists in Paris when he lived in the city in the 1920s: Pablo Picasso, James Joyce, F. Scott Fitzgerald, and Gertrude Stein, to name a few. He had worked as an ambulance driver on the Italian front in World War I and was awarded the Italian War Merit Cross for his bravery. His novel *For Whom the Bell Tolls* (1940) is about the Spanish Civil War, in which Hemingway fought, supporting the resistance against General Francisco Franco. He earned the Bronze Star for his work as a war reporter during World War II. He later backed the revolutionaries led by Fidel Castro, who overthrew the corrupt government in Cuba. Hemingway won both the Pulitzer Prize and the Nobel Prize for Literature.

I loved reading *For Whom the Bell Tolls*, and that interest, naturally, led me to the poem of the same name by John Donne, an Elizabethan poet born in 1572. Donne is regarded as the pre-eminent representative of metaphysical poets (those who emphasise ideas, and the spoken rather than lyrical quality of their verse). He has been described by critic Katherine Rundell as 'the greatest writer of desire in the English language'. He was also an MP for the constituency of Brackley in West Northamptonshire from 1601 to 1614.

When I first read the poem, it made me feel quite emotional. Donne's verse embodies my belief that we need an awareness of the plight of all human beings throughout the world and the common bonds we share.

∽

No man is an island,
Entire of itself.
Each is a piece of the continent,
A part of the main.
If a clod be washed away by the sea,
Europe is the less.
As well as if a promontory were.
As well as if a manor of thine own
Or of thine friend's were.
Each man's death diminishes me,
For I am involved in mankind.
Therefore, send not to know
For whom the bell tolls,
It tolls for thee.

∽

sorrow song

LUCILLE CLIFTON (1939–2010)

Selected by Jeremy

Maya Angelou, June Jordan and Lucille Clifton are among the most influential Black female poets of the twentieth century.

Maya Angelou was an inspiration. Her poetry speaks of empowerment, struggle, and the fight to survive, words that reflect her life—a child sent away by estranged parents, who received a mixed and incomplete education, with deep determination to do anything that felt like herself, be that as a dancer, croupier, writer, teacher, activist or organiser. A confidante of Martin Luther King and Malcom X, she was devastated by their successive assassinations. Over time, she became a figure in the U.S. Democratic establishment. President Obama invited her to read a poem at the Democratic National Convention. Her book, *I Know Why the Caged Bird Sings*, published in 1969, was the first in a seven-volume autobiography. Her third volume of poetry, *And Still I Rise*, was published in 1978. The poem that gave the book its title, 'Still I Rise', is extraordinarily moving. I have heard it read many times, most memorably by Dawn Butler at the Labour Women's Conference in Telford in 2018. It received a lengthy standing ovation.

Poetry is key to political empowerment, and provides hope, education, and defiance. June Jordan was a prolific writer. She produced twenty-seven volumes of poems and became one of the most widely published and highly acclaimed Jamaican American writers of her generation, Born July 9, 1936, in Harlem, New York, Jordan also had a difficult childhood and an especially fraught relationship with her father. She wrote of her experiences growing up and encouraged others to do the same. This culminated in her 1970 book *The Voices of the Children*, in which she inspired twenty Black children to write their poetic impressions of growing up in the ghettos of America. A lifelong campaigner, she was known for her fierce commitment to human rights. In an interview with *Colorlines* magazine she insisted that 'poetry is a political act because it involves telling the truth'.

For our book I have chosen a poem by Lucille Clifton 'sorrow song'. Clifton was born in 1936 in Depew, New York. She was discovered as a poet by Langston Hughes and featured in his highly influential anthology, *The Poetry of the Negro*. Her work emphasizes endurance and strength through adversity, focusing particularly on African American experience and family life. In addition to her numerous poetry collections, she was the author of many children's books. She wrote about her heroes, including nameless slaves buried on old plantations, the first child killed in the Soweto riot (Hector Pieterson), Nelson Mandela, and many other people who gave their lives to free Black people from slavery and prejudice. 'sorrow song' is a devastating indictment of war, considering the perspective of its young victims.

for the eyes of the children,
the last to melt,
the last to vaporize,
for the lingering
eyes of the children, staring,
the eyes of the children of

buchenwald,
of viet nam and johannesburg,
for the eyes of the children
of nagasaki,
for the eyes of the children
of middle passage,
for cherokee eyes, ethiopian eyes,
russian eyes, american eyes,
for all that remains of the children,
their eyes,
staring at us, amazed to see
the extraordinary evil in
ordinary men.

The Runaway Slave at Pilgrim's Point
ELIZABETH BARRETT BROWNING (1806–1861)
Selected by Jeremy

Elizabeth Barrett Browning was a prolific poet, a deep thinker, and an acute observer of life around her. She was interested in literature from a young age—by twelve, she had written her first poem. Barrett Browning's family owned a sugar plantation in Jamaica and amassed most of their wealth from the slave trade. In rebellion against her family and their riches, Barrett Browning campaigned to end slavery and became engaged to a man of whom her father disapproved. After she married Robert Browning in 1846, Barrett Browning's family disowned her. She and Robert, also a poet, struggled financially. They lived in Italy, where Barrett Browning died in 1861.

Barrett Browning became dedicated to many causes, including factory legislation and abolishing slavery. Her poem 'The Runaway Slave at Pilgrim's Point' was written in 1846. The poem originally appeared in *Liberty Bell*, an abolitionist gift book. It is such a sad and terrible poem one can't help but wonder how those who gained wealth and power from the slave trade would have reacted to it. In addition to poems about social justice, Barrett Browning wrote poetry about love, romance, and nature.

After William Wordsworth's death in 1850, Barrett Browning was considered as a successor for the poet laureateship, but instead, Alfred Tennyson, who wrote "safe" poems that did little to trouble the deeply insecure sycophants of early Victorian Britain, was named the laureate.

Although Barrett Browning is less well-known than the writers she influenced, such as Emily Dickinson, her work had a massive impact while she was alive and an even greater one after her death.

I stand on the mark beside the shore
Of the first white pilgrim's bended knee,
Where exile turned to ancestor,
And God was thanked for liberty.
I have run through the night, my skin is as dark,
I bend my knee down on this mark:
I look on the sky and the sea.

O pilgrim-souls, I speak to you!
I see you come out proud and slow
From the land of the spirits pale as dew
And round me and round me ye go.
O pilgrims, I have gasped and run
All night long from the whips of one
Who in your names works sin and woe!

And thus I thought that I would come
And kneel here where ye knelt before,
And feel your souls around me hum
In undertone to the ocean's roar;
And lift my black face, my black hand,
Here, in your names, to curse this land
Ye blessed in freedom's, evermore.

I am black, I am black;
And yet God made me, they say:

But if He did so, smiling back
He must have cast His work away
Under the feet of His white creatures,
With a look of scorn, that the dusky features
Might be trodden again to clay.

And yet He has made dark things
To be glad and merry as light:
There's a little dark bird sits and sings,
There's a dark stream ripples out of sight,
And the dark frogs chant in the safe morass,
And the sweetest stars are made to pass
O'er the face of the darkest night.

But *we* who are dark, we are dark!
Ah God, we have no stars!
About our souls in care and cark
Our blackness shuts like prison-bars:
The poor souls crouch so far behind,
That never a comfort can they find
By reaching through the prison-bars.

Indeed, we live beneath the sky,
That great smooth Hand of God stretched out
On all His children fatherly,
To save them from the fear and doubt
Which would be if, from this low place,
All opened straight up to His face
Into the grand eternity.

And still God's sunshine and His frost,
They make us hot; they make us cold,
As if we were not black and lost;

And the beasts and birds, in wood and fold,
Do fear and take us for very men!
Could the whip-poor-will or the cat of the glen
Look into my eyes and be bold?

I am black, I am black!
But, once, I laughed in girlish glee;
For one of my colour stood in the track
Where the drivers drove, and looked at me,
And tender and full was the look he gave—
Could a slave look *so* at another slave?—
I look at the sky and the sea.

And from that hour our spirits grew
As free as if unsold, unbought:
Oh, strong enough, since we were two
To conquer the world, we thought.
The drivers drove us day by day;
We did not mind, we went one way,
And no better a freedom sought.

In the sunny ground between the canes,
He said "I love you" as he passed:
When the shingle-roof rang sharp with the rains,
I heard how he vowed it fast:
While others shook, he smiled in the hut,
As he carved me a bowl of the cocoa-nut
Through the roar of the hurricanes.

I sang his name instead of a song,
Over and over I sang his name,
Upward and downward I drew it along
My various notes,—the same, the same!

I sang it low, that the slave-girls near
Might never guess, from aught they could hear,
It was only a name—a name.

I look on the sky and the sea.
We were two to love, and two to pray:
Yes, two, O God, who cried to Thee,
Though nothing didst Thou say!
Coldly Thou sat'st behind the sun:
And now I cry who am but one,
Thou wilt not speak to-day.

We were black, we were black,
We had no claim to love and bliss,
What marvel, if each went to wrack?
They wrung my cold hands out of his
They dragged him—where ? I crawled to touch
His blood's mark in the dust . . . not much,
Ye pilgrim-souls, . . . though plain as *this!*

Wrong, followed by a deeper wrong!
Mere grief's too good for such as I:
So the white men brought the shame ere long
To strangle the sob of my agony.
They would not leave me for my dull
Wet eyes! —it was too merciful
To let me weep pure tears and die.

I am black, I am black!
I wore a child upon my breast
An amulet that hung too slack,
And, in my unrest, could not rest:
Thus we went moaning, child and mother,

One to another, one to another,
Until all ended for the best.

For hark! I will tell you low, low,
I am black, you see,—
And the babe who lay on my bosom so,
Was far too white, too white for me;
As white as the ladies who scorned to pray
Beside me at church but yesterday,
Though my tears had washed a place for my knee.

My own, own child! I could not bear
To look in his face, it was so white;
I covered him up with a kerchief there,
I covered his face in close and tight:
And he moaned and struggled, as well might be,
For the white child wanted his liberty—
Ha, ha! he wanted his master-right.

He moaned and beat with his head and feet,
His little feet that never grew;
He struck them out, as it was meet,
Against my heart to break it through:
I might have sung and made him mild,
But I dared not sing to the white-faced child
The only song I knew.

I pulled the kerchief very close:
He could not see the sun, I swear,
More, then, alive, than now he does
From between the roots of the mango . . . where?
I know where. Close! A child and mother

Do wrong to look at one another
When one is black and one is fair.

Why, in that single glance I had
Of my child's face, . . . I tell you all,
I saw a look that made me mad!
The *master's* look, that used to fall
On my soul like his lash . . . or worse!
And so, to save it from my curse,
I twisted it round in my shawl.

And he moaned and trembled from foot to head,
He shivered from head to foot;
Till after a time, he lay instead
Too suddenly still and mute.
I felt, beside, a stiffening cold:
I dared to lift up just a fold,
As in lifting a leaf of the mango-fruit.

But *my* fruit . . . ha, ha!—there, had been
(I laugh to think on't at this hour!)
Your fine white angels (who have seen
Nearest the secret of God's power)
And plucked my fruit to make them wine,
And sucked the soul of that child of mine
As the humming-bird sucks the soul of the flower.

Ha, ha, the trick of the angels white!
They freed the white child's spirit so.
I said not a word, but day and night,
I carried the body to and fro,

And it lay on my heart like a stone, as chill.
—The sun may shine out as much as he will:
I am cold, though it happened a month ago.

From the white man's house, and the black man's hut,
I carried the little body on;
The forest's arms did round us shut,
And silence through the trees did run:
They asked no question as I went,
They stood too high for astonishment,
They could see God sit on His throne.

My little body, kerchiefed fast,
I bore it on through the forest, on;
And when I felt it was tired at last,
I scooped a hole beneath the moon:
Through the forest-tops the angels far,
With a white sharp finger from every star,
Did point and mock at what was done.

Yet when it was all done aright,—
Earth, 'twixt me and my baby, strewed—
All, changed to black earth,—nothing white,—
A dark child in the dark!—ensued
Some comfort, and my heart grew young;
I sate down smiling there and sung
The song I learnt in my maidenhood.

And thus we two were reconciled,
The white child and black mother, thus:
For as I sang it soft and wild,
The same song, more melodious,
Rose from the grave whereon I sate:

It was the dead child singing that,
To join the souls of both of us.

I look on the sea and the sky.
Where the pilgrims' ships first anchored lay
The free sun rideth gloriously,
But the pilgrim-ghosts have slid away
Through the earliest streaks of the morn:
My face is black, but it glares with a scorn
Which they dare not meet by day.

Ha!—in their stead, their hunter sons!
Ha, ha! they are on me—they hunt in a ring!
Keep off! I brave you all at once,
I throw off your eyes like snakes that sting!
You have killed the black eagle at nest, I think:
Did you ever stand still in your triumph, and shrink
From the stroke of her wounded wing?

(Man, drop that stone you dared to lift!—)
I wish you who stand there five abreast,
Each, for his own wife's joy and gift,
A little corpse as safely at rest
As mine in the mangos! Yes, but *she*
May keep live babies on her knee,
And sing the song she likes the best.

I am not mad: I am black.
I see you staring in my face—
I know you, staring, shrinking back,
Ye are born of the Washington-race,
And this land is the free America,
And this mark on my wrist— (I prove what I say)

Ropes tied me up here to the flogging-place.

You think I shrieked then? Not a sound!
I hung, as a gourd hangs in the sun;
I only cursed them all around,
As softly as I might have done
My very own child: from these sands
Up to the mountains, lift your hands,
O slaves, and end what I begun!

Whips, curses; these must answer those!
For in this UNION you have set
Two kinds of men in adverse rows,
Each loathing each; and all forget
The seven wounds in Christ's body fair;
While HE sees gaping everywhere
Our countless wounds that pay no debt.

Our wounds are different. Your white men
Are, after all, not gods indeed,
Nor able to make Christs again
Do good with bleeding. *We* who bleed
(Stand off!) we help not in our loss!
We are too heavy for our cross,
And fall and crush you and your seed.

I fall, I swoon! I look at the sky.
The clouds are breaking on my brain;
I am floated along, as if I should die
Of liberty's exquisite pain.

In the name of the white child waiting for me
In the death-dark where we may kiss and agree,
White men, I leave you all curse-free
In my broken heart's disdain!

Home

WARSAN SHIRE (1988–)

Selected by Jeremy

This poem is so real. It is a vital message of and for our times. 'Home' is an utterly brilliant description of the desperation of refugees, as well as the racism and loneliness that follows after starting a new life.

The European politicians of the twenty-first century will not be treated well by history. Their response to the refugee crisis—caused by wars, poverty, oppression, and environmental disaster—has been terrible. The vast majority of the world's refugees and displaced people are accommodated in countries that are often equally as poor as the places from which refugees are leaving. The small number of refugees who do try to enter Europe are met by barbed wire and police surveillance.

Warsan Shire's poetry often focuses on empowering people, particularly young Black women. 'Home' is about Black refugees who are widely ignored in the media.

Shire was born in Kenya to Somali parents. She grew up in London, and much of her poetry is about reconciling different notions of home. In an interview from 2013 she said, 'I grew up with a lot of horror in the backdrop—a lot of terrible things that have happened to people who are really close to me, and to my country, and to my parents; so it's in the home and it's even in you, it's on your skin and it's in your memories and your childhood.' Her anthology, *Bless the Daughter Raised by a Voice in Her Head* (2022), is an amazing collection of poetry that she modestly characterises as an exploration of feelings and our world. Shire explains that her poems always describe someone she knows or has met. Her work demonstrates the power of poetry to inspire.

∽

I

No one leaves home unless home is the mouth of a shark. You only run for the border when you see the whole city running as well. The boy you went to school with, who kissed you dizzy behind the old tin factory, is holding a gun bigger than his body. You only leave home when home won't let you stay.

No one would leave home unless home chased you. It's not something you ever thought about doing, so when you did, you carried the anthem under your breath, waiting until the airport toilet to tear up the passport and swallow, each mournful mouthful making it clear you would not be going back.

No one puts their children in a boat, unless the water is safer than the land. No one would choose days and nights in the stomach of a truck, unless the miles travelled meant something more than journey.

No one would choose to crawl under fences, beaten until your shadow leaves, raped, forced off the boat because you are darker, drowned, sold, starved, shot at the border like a sick animal, pitied. No one would choose to make a refugee camp home for a year or two or ten, stripped and searched, finding prison everywhere. And if you were to survive, greeted on the other side—*Go home Blacks, dirty refugees, sucking our country dry of milk, dark with their hands out, smell strange, savage, look what they've done to their own countries, what will they do to ours?*

The insults are easier to swallow than finding your child's body in the rubble.

I want to go home, but home is the mouth of a shark. Home is the barrel of a gun. No one would leave home unless home chased you to the shore. No one would leave home until home is a voice in your ear saying—*leave, run, now. I don't know what I've become.*

II

I don't know where I'm going. Where I came from is disappearing. I am unwelcome. My beauty is not beauty here. My body is burning with the shame of not belonging, my body is longing. I am the sin of memory and the absence of memory. I watch the news and my mouth becomes a sink full of blood. The lines, forms, people at the desks, calling cards, immigration officers, the looks on the street, the cold settling deep into my bones, the English classes at night, the distance I am from home. Alhamdulillah, all of this is better than the scent of a woman completely on fire, a truckload of men who look like my father—pulling out my teeth and nails. All these men between my legs, a gun, a promise, a lie, his name, his flag, his language, his manhood in my mouth.

∼

His Hands Were Gentle

ADRIAN MITCHELL (1932–2008)

Selected by Jeremy

Víctor Jara was assassinated on September 16, 1973, in a soccer stadium in Santiago, Chile. He was brutally beaten and then shot by the forces of Chilean dictator Augusto Pinochet. Jara's death happened shortly after Pinochet's coup, which overthrew the democratically elected government of Salvador Allende, a socialist who was also murdered by Pinochet's men and was buried in the same cemetery as Jara.

Jara is remembered all over the world for his inspiring music. He was one of the creators of the *nueva canción* movement and genre, which consists of leftist, politically charged popular songs.

Adrian Mitchell's 'His Hands Were Gentle' is a lovely tribute to Jara, whose whole life was one of political song, activism, and inspiration. While trapped in the soccer stadium alongside thousands of other members of Popular Unity (Allende's party), Jara tried to sing 'Venceremos' ('We Shall Overcome'), the song of the party. Infuriated, the soldiers guarding those in the stadium smashed his hands, preventing him from playing his beloved guitar. The soldiers used Jara as an example to intimidate the others incarcerated in the stadium, but his spirit was not broken, so they shot him dead.

His widow, Joan Jara, managed to escape from Chile after the coup. She came to London, where she was looked after by Adrian and Celia Mitchell, who were enormously active in supporting the Chile Solidarity Campaign. Its offices were at the Red Rose Centre in my North Islington constituency. Joan lived a short distance away on Kiver Road.

After the removal of Pinochet in 1990 and during the Cambio de Mano (Change of Hand), Joan returned to Chile. Very late at night on the day of the handover from Pinochet to President Patricio Aylwin, she and I went to La Población La Victoria, a poor community in Santiago where Jara had been an inspiration and continues to be one.

This song describes the life and death of Jara. Mitchell also wrote brilliant anti-war poetry. His famous stanza, 'Tell Me Lies about Vietnam', was later adapted to oppose the Iraq War in 2003, 'Tell Me Lies about Iraq.' Mitchell once said, 'most people ignore most poetry because poetry ignores most people'. Accordingly, he wrote popular poetry for peace. Arlo Guthrie, who first performed 'Tell Me Lies about Vietnam' in 1976, has also been a lifelong voice for peace.

Victor Jara of Chile
Lived like a shooting star
He fought for the people of Chile
With his songs and his guitar
His hands were gentle, his hands were strong

Victor Jara was a peasant
He worked from a few years old
He sat upon his father's plow
And watched the earth unfold
His hands were gentle, his hands were strong

Now when the neighbors had a wedding
Or one of their children died

His mother sang all night for them
With Victor by her side
His hands were gentle, his hands were strong

He grew up to be a fighter
Against the people's wrongs
He listened to their grief and joy
And turned them into songs
His hands were gentle, his hands were strong

He sang about the copper miners
And those who worked the land
He sang about the factory workers
And they knew he was their man
His hands were gentle, his hands were strong

He campaigned for Allende
Working night and day
He sang 'Take hold of your brother's hand
You know the future begins today'
His hands were gentle, his hands were strong

Then the generals seized Chile
They arrested Victor then
They caged him in a stadium
With five thousand frightened men
His hands were gentle, his hands were strong

Victor stood in the stadium
His voice was brave and strong
And he sang for his fellow prisoners
Till the guards cut short his song
His hands were gentle, his hands were strong

They broke the bones in both his hands
They beat him on the head
They tore him with electric shocks
And then they shot him dead
His hands were gentle, his hands were strong

Bread and Roses

JAMES OPPENHEIM (1882–1932)

Selected by Len

'Bread and Roses' is a wonderful slogan, pairing with brilliant simplicity the right not just to what is necessary to live, but also to life's beauty and pleasure. It is well-known around the radical movements of the world. It was first used at the turn of the last century in relation to trade union and political struggles.

It was Helen Todd, a great American feminist, who coined the phrase 'We want bread for all, and roses too' in her 1910 speech about women's suffrage. The phrase became the soul of the women's rights movement fighting for universal suffrage and equality. The sentiment was also at the centre of the 1912 Lawrence Textile Strike in Massachusetts. Known as the Bread and Roses Strike, it was an industrial action that shook America.

From January to March, during the bitter cold winter, tens of thousands of textile workers came out on strike. Women and children were beaten indiscriminately by police, causing national outrage. After nine weeks, the union, the Industrial Workers of the World (IWW), won a pay rise of 15 to 20 percent, plus improvements in overtime rates and conditions. The strike also led to approximately 275,000 textile workers in New England getting similar increases from other companies who were fearful of the IWW calling strikes in their factories too.

Nearly eighty years later, another famous bread and roses strike took place in Los Angeles. The Service Employees International Union (SEIU) was engaged in the Justice for Janitors Campaign, seeking fair pay and treatment for the mainly Latino workers. Just as in 1912 in Massachusetts, the police disrupted a peaceful march by violently attacking the demonstrators. This horrified many people across America, and their subsequent support for the demonstrators led to the successful recognition of the union and the settlement of its demands. Ken Loach's film, *Bread and Roses*, depicts brilliantly the Los Angeles strike.

For thirty years I have had a close relationship with the SEIU leadership, and Unite has learned much from their campaigning methods. The SEIU slogan, 'Fighting for the invisible workers,' was so resonant—invisible because these are the men and women who come into our workplace when we have gone home and leave it spotless for when we arrive at work the following day.

James Oppenheim's 1911 poem superbly captures the meaning and spirit of the slogan 'Bread and Roses'.

As we come marching, marching, in the beauty of the day,
A million darkened kitchens, a thousand mill-lofts gray
Are touched with all the radiance that a sudden sun discloses,
For the people hear us singing, "Bread and Roses, Bread and Roses."

As we come marching, marching, we battle, too, for men—
For they are women's children and we mother them again.
Our lives shall not be sweated from birth until life closes—
Hearts starve as well as bodies: Give us Bread, but give us Roses!

As we come marching, marching, unnumbered women dead
Go crying through our singing their ancient song of Bread;
Small art and love and beauty their drudging spirits knew—
Yes, bread we fight for—but we fight for Roses, too.

As we come marching, marching, we bring the Greater Days—
The rising of the women means the rising of the race—
No more the drudge and idler—ten that toil where one reposes—
But a sharing of life's glories: Bread and Roses, Bread and Roses!

Scotland, You're No Mine

HANNAH LAVERY (1977–)

Selected by Jeremy

Hannah Lavery is a poet, playwright, and theater director. I was introduced to her work at the Edinburgh Festival and Book Fair in 2022. She had just been installed as Edinburgh's Makar (poet laureate). Len and I hosted an event at the festival where, crammed into a sweltering basement room, we read poems and discussed poets with a wonderful, engaged audience.

I chose this poem because I wanted to pay homage to the flowering of books and poetry that is occurring in modern Scotland, especially among the young.

Lavery is a young Scottish woman of colour. Hers is a voice that speaks to and for the conflicted conscience of Scotland around issues of identity, race, justice, and belonging. Her writing is both powerful and authentic. Her play *Lament for Sheku Bayoh* is based on the real-life story of a Black thirty-one-year-old father of two who died in police custody on the streets of his hometown of Kirkcaldy, Fife, in 2015. It portrays injustice in a powerful and thought-provoking manner.

Lavery's poem 'Scotland, You're No Mine' is best described in her own words: 'I wrote this poem in a breath. A long-held breath. All that was long held, for so long, was coughed and spat out on the page. There is rage here, much rage, at Scotland's amnesia, at her claims of exceptionalism, but this is a love song, too. A complicated love song, of an often-unrequited love, but still, with all its bile and pain, this is an expression of love. My love song for my country, for my home and for where I belong.'

The love of people and place, the irritation at excessive nationalism, and the contradictory feelings about Scotland and its history and future; all these elements are represented in Lavery's poem. It veers between youthful contempt and love and appreciation of the joys of Scotland. It was published in 2019 as part of her book, *Finding Seaglass*.

When I recited this poem at the festival, I was conscious of the colloquial language but did not want to edit it. After, I was greeted by a group of friends who had attended the event with their ninety-one-year-old grandmother. They complimented the poem and we all agreed on its honest portrayal of rage and love.

Scotland, you're no mine
(you were no his)
and I don't want you.

So go ahead, say I don't belong,
wi your sepia-tinged cross eye sweeping
over all that swept-away, blood-stained, sweat-
        stained sugar for your tablet.

Ya macaroon. Ya rotten,
gobby, greedy, thieving bastard you,
sitting atop a that shite and broken bones, weeping,
        Poor me.

Fuck you! I will dance jigs on your flags
blue n white; blue, white n red.
It doesne matter but, ya wee chancer!

Fuck! For making us complicit,
handing us whip and chains, an officer's coat,
a civil-service pen, a Queen to love.

And lay me out, I love you
with your mountain thyme and all your coorie in.
And you can say, I dinnae belong to you—go on

—but I am limpet stuck on you.
So fuck you for no seeing one of your own.
I will, here. I will spill, here,

my blood and your secrets,
bleed into you, root and earth,
and you, forever, pagan, will, in the spill

and the seep, see all you really are.
So fuck you, my sweet forgetful Caledonia.
With love, fuck you.

Various Love Poems

Selected by Len

Poetry touches every emotion, and one of the most powerful is love. Countless poets have dealt with the wonders and joys of love, the pain of lost love, the hurt of rejection.

I am deeply drawn to love poems and songs. Perhaps it's the romantic in me. Here, I have chosen five love poems from the many I admire.

Love's Philosophy, Percy Bysshe Shelley (1792–1822) One of the great Romantics, he was also a radical in his political views and his lifestyle. Incredibly, he did not achieve fame in his lifetime. Now regarded as one of the greatest poets, he died tragically in a sailing accident in Italy at the age of just twenty-nine.

She Walks in Beauty, Lord Byron (1788–1824) Lord Byron, like his friend Shelley, was a leading poet in the Romantic movement. He led a colourful life, spending seven years in Italy. He fought and died in the Greek War of Independence against the Ottoman Empire. He was thirty-six years old.

On Love, Kahlil Gibran (1883–1931) Gibran was a Lebanese-American poet who died at age forty-eight. He was considered a rebel by conservative authorities and is revered in Lebanon. His major work, 'The Prophet', encompasses twenty-six beautiful poetic meditations on various subjects.

When You Are Old, William Butler Yeats (1865–1939) Yeats was one of the poets responsible for the Irish literary revival and Irish National Theatre Society. His influences included Percy Bysshe

Shelley, William Blake, and Oscar Wilde. He was a longtime friend of Countess Markiewicz, the socialist, revolutionary, and nationalist who was the first woman elected to the Westminster parliament in 1918. Yeats himself was a nationalist but had issues with some of the leaders of the Republican movement and their tactics. The Easter Rising in 1916 made him reassess his attitude and his failure to recognise the merits of the nationalist leadership. In his poem 'Easter, 1916' he wrote:

> I write it out in a verse—
> MacDonagh and MacBride
> And Connolly and Pearse
> Now and in time to be,
> Wherever green is worn,
> Are changed, changed utterly:
> A terrible beauty is born.

Sonnet XVIII ('Shall I compare thee to a summer's day'), William Shakespeare (1564–1616) Shakespeare is regarded by many as the greatest English poet. For decades scholars have discussed who this sonnet was written for, and many have concluded it was for a young man. All I know is it's one love to another.

Love's Philosophy
PERCY BYSSHE SHELLEY

The fountains mingle with the river
    And the rivers with the ocean,
The winds of heaven mix for ever
    With a sweet emotion;

Nothing in the world is single;
    All things by a law divine
In one spirit meet and mingle.
    Why not I with thine?—

See the mountains kiss high heaven
    And the waves clasp one another;
No sister-flower would be forgiven
    If it disdained its brother;
And the sunlight clasps the earth
    And the moonbeams kiss the sea:
What is all this sweet work worth
    If thou kiss not me?

She Walks in Beauty
LORD BYRON

She walks in beauty, like the night
Of cloudless climes and starry skies;
And all that's best of dark and bright
Meet in her aspect and her eyes:
Thus mellow'd to that tender light
Which heaven to gaudy day denies.

One shade the more, one ray the less,
Had half impaired the nameless grace
Which waves in every raven tress,
Or softly lightens o'er her face;

Where thoughts serenely sweet express
How pure, how dear their dwelling-place.

And on that cheek, and o'er that brow,
So soft, so calm, yet eloquent,
The smiles that win, the tints that glow,
But tell of days in goodness spent,
A mind at peace with all below,
A heart whose love is innocent!

On Love
KAHLIL GIBRAN

Then said Almitra, Speak to us of Love.
    And he raised his head and looked upon the people, and there fell a stillness upon them. And with a great voice he said:
    When love beckons to you, follow him,
    Though his ways are hard and steep.
    And when his wings enfold you yield to him,
    Though the sword hidden among his pinions may wound you.
    And when he speaks to you believe in him,
    Though his voice may shatter your dreams as the north wind lays waste the garden.

    For even as love crowns you so shall he crucify you. Even as he is for your growth

so is he for your pruning.
   Even as he ascends to your height and caresses your tenderest branches that quiver in the sun,
   So shall he descend to your roots and shake them in their clinging to the earth.

•

   Like sheaves of corn he gathers you unto himself.
He threshes you to make you naked.
He sifts you to free you from your husks.
He grinds you to whiteness.
He kneads you until you are pliant;
   And then he assigns you to his sacred fire, that you may become sacred bread for God's sacred feast.

   All these things shall love do unto you that you may know the secrets of your heart, and in that knowledge become a fragment of Life's heart.

   But if in your fear you would seek only love's peace and love's pleasure,
   Then it is better for you that you cover your nakedness and pass out of love's threshing-floor,
   Into the seasonless world where you shall laugh, but not all of your laughter, and weep, but not all of your tears.

•

Love gives naught but itself and takes naught but from itself.

Love possesses not nor would it be possessed;

For love is sufficient unto love.

When you love you should not say, "God is in my heart," but rather, "I am in the heart of God."

And think not you can direct the course of love, for love, if it finds you worthy, directs your course.

Love has no other desire but to fulfil itself.

But if you love and must needs have desires, let these be your desires:

To melt and be like a running brook that sings its melody to the night.

To know the pain of too much tenderness.

To be wounded by your own understanding of love;

And to bleed willingly and joyfully.

To wake at dawn with a winged heart and give thanks for another day of loving;

To rest at the noon hour and meditate love's ecstasy;

To return home at eventide with gratitude;

And then to sleep with a prayer for the beloved in your heart and a song of praise upon your lips.

When You Are Old
WILLIAM BUTLER YEATS

When you are old and grey and full of sleep,
And nodding by the fire, take down this book,
And slowly read, and dream of the soft look
Your eyes had once, and of their shadows deep;

How many loved your moments of glad grace,
And loved your beauty with love false or true,
But one man loved the pilgrim soul in you,
And loved the sorrows of your changing face;

And bending down beside the glowing bars,
Murmur, a little sadly, how Love fled
And paced upon the mountains overhead
And hid his face amid a crowd of stars.

Sonnet XVIII
WILLIAM SHAKESPEARE

Shall I compare thee to a summer's day?
Thou art more lovely and more temperate.
Rough winds do shake the darling buds of May,
And summer's lease hath all too short a date.
Sometime too hot the eye of heaven shines,
And often is his gold complexion dimmed;
And every fair from fair sometime declines,
By chance, or nature's changing course, untrimmed;
But thy eternal summer shall not fade,

Nor lose possession of that fair thou ow'st,
Nor shall death brag thou wand'rest in his shade,
When in eternal lines to Time thou grow'st.
   So long as men can breathe, or eyes can see,
   So long lives this, and this gives life to thee.

The Incandescence of the Wind

BEN OKRI (1959–)

Selected by Jeremy

Ben Okri is one of our great global writers. His list of publications is extensive, but, for me, his novel *The Famished Road* is especially brilliant.

The book is evocative of Okri's country of birth, Nigeria, on the verge of independence, replete with the traumas caused by urbanisation's chaotic and brutal spread, and its once plentiful and bountiful forests that were rapidly eaten away and destroyed.

'The most authentic thing about us is our capacity to create, to overcome, to endure, to transform, to love' is an Okri line I quoted in my speech to the Labour Party Conference in 2015. He kindly wrote and thanked me for it. He did not need to; it was my pleasure and honour.

In July 2016 the two us appeared on the stage of London's Royal Festival Hall in front of a large audience to talk about and read from poetry and books that meant a great deal to us. We focused especially on the contrast between the influence of European literature on Africa and African literature on Europe. We felt that, for it to work, the proceedings needed to be spontaneous, so we did not rehearse. Others are in a better position to judge than I, but it seemed to go well.

Two years later Okri published his book *Rise Like Lions: Poetry for the Many*—I think the title was influenced by the 2017 election campaign. In it, Okri republished a poem he had written in 1982, 'The Incandescence of the Wind'.

1982 was only a few years after the conflict in Biafra and was a time when Nigeria was going through multiple coups and successive military governments. The poem describes fear, power, and the ephemeral nature of authority and the way it is exercised behind tinted glass offices, remote from the destruction, killing, and horror of conflict.

The last lines of the poem poignantly describe the way conflict and war live on and change our psyche.

> — a new spirit breathing phosphorous
> has grown
> into the blue roots of the times.

~

The incandescence of the wind
bothers me
in this vineyard.
Is there a searing clarity
about the noises
rising daily
from this riverbed we call our own?

The yam-tubers bleed our sorrows.
Crows in the fields
scream of despair.
Machetes pollute our food
with rust.
The masters conduct their
plunderings
with quiet murders:

The victims perform maypole dances
around the village shrines.

There is a cold fire in the air.
I hear it
consume the groins
of heroes
and shrivel the guts
of martyrs.
The name of the fire
is printed on grave stones:
names squeezed for tubers of life
and collective cowardice.

At night mothers scream
of children lost in the city fires
of children lost in neon signs
and cellars of madness.
I hear noises from the streets:

men are lost in files
or have wandered
into the fractured severity
of military gun-shots
have become a generation
drenched in petrol
camp-fired
and barbequed
in the fevers
of elections
riots
coups.

The incandescence in the air
burns inward.
Is there a name for this fear?
Is there a fearful country
in these fields
where such realities are
manufactured whole?

I heard a secret
in the burning iron of the mornings.
Animals
have delivered eggs of blood.
Women
have discovered the secret
of an inviolable flesh-haze.
There are multiple deaths
in the riverbeds
polluting our world
with an irascible sense
of failure.
Shall we join them
or shall we celebrate
the vision of empty offices
the short-sightedness of power.

Break the bread
of initiation into revolt:
We shall celebrate with our
emaciated chests.
We shall clench and raise our fists
in the wonder of incandescence.

I hear a light
bursting up through
the bright blue roots
and the yellow skeletons.
We have breathed
our self-love in those bones.
We have breathed
incantations
at those worms
that ravage our serenity.

The graveyards heave.
The riverbeds sigh.
And I wake surprised:
    – the incandescence has become
our own
    – the skeletons have reclaimed
the lands
    – a new spirit breathing phosphorous
has grown
into the blue roots of the times.

∽

Scots Wha Hae

ROBERT (RABBIE) BURNS (1759–1796)

Selected by Len

Scotland has always held a special place in my heart. Not only because of my love of Liverpool Football Club, whose legendary manager Bill Shankly recruited some of its greatest players, notably Ron Yeats and my first hero, Ian St John, from north of the border, but also because Scotland, like Liverpool, has always been a bastion of fierce independence and radical thought.

Until the Labour Party took the Scottish working class for granted, Scotland was also always a Red nation, a Labour stronghold. At that point, people turned to the Scottish National Party, seen as a more radical social democratic party. The only way to win the Scottish working class back is for Labour to rediscover its own radical edge.

We often looked to Scotland to understand the great industrial issues of our time; for example, the workers' occupation of the Upper Clyde shipyards (UCS) in 1971, led by Jimmy Reid, was simply incredible. During the dispute, Reid came to the Liverpool docks to speak. Listening to him made the hair on the back of my neck stand up; I was twenty-one years old. When I became general secretary of Unite, I had the privilege of making the inaugural address at the Jimmy Reid Foundation.

In many ways it was inevitable that I would seek out the poetry of Scotland's Bard (the national poet), Rabbie Burns. Burns grew up impoverished and in great hardship. Working on his family's tenanted farm left its mark; he died at only thirty-seven (although some said alcohol helped him on his way, too).

Burns was an inspiration for those who founded the liberal and socialist movements. He became an icon in Scotland, and in a Scottish TV poll he was voted the greatest Scot ever. He was radical in his views and was a supporter of the French Revolution and the American War of Independence. Burns Night (on or near his birthday, January 25) is celebrated all over the world and is my favourite night of the year.

Rabbie Burns' prolific work is incredible. Who knows what he would have produced had his life not been prematurely cut short. He wrote the words to 'Auld Lang Syne', which must be the most sung song in the world after 'Happy Birthday', as well as many well-known poems: 'A Red, Red Rose'; 'A Man's a Man for A' That'; 'To a Mouse'; 'Ae Fond Kiss'; and his masterpiece, 'Tam o' Shanter'.

I have chosen here what was, for many years, the unofficial national anthem of Scotland: 'Scots Wha Hae'.

Scots, wha hae wi' Wallace bled,
Scots, wham Bruce has aften led;
Welcome to your gory bed,
    Or to victory!

Now's the day, and now's the hour;
See the front o' battle lour;
See approach proud Edward's power—
    Chains and slavery!

Wha will be a traitor knave?
Wha can fill a coward's grave!

Wha sae base as be a slave?
    Let him turn and flee!

Wha for Scotland's king and law
Freedom's sword will strongly draw,
Freeman stand, or freeman fa',
    Let him follow me!

By oppression's woes and pains!
By your sons in servile chains!
We will drain our dearest veins,
    But they shall be free!

Lay the proud usurpers low!
Tyrants fall in every foe!
Liberty's in every blow!—
    Let us do or die!

A Prison Daybreak

FAIZ AHMED FAIZ (1911–1984)

Selected by Jeremy

Poems and their meanings are specific to the language of the author. Translating poetry is difficult. A poem that rhymes in English will not have the same effect in another language. Author and translator Naomi Lazard described the process of translating Faiz Ahmed Faiz's work as a lengthy one, involving numerous discussions with him before being able to convey the Urdu meaning in English.

Faiz was editor of the *Pakistan Times*. He always wrote in a way that advocated for peace and spoke up for the oppressed poor and the illiterate people in Pakistan. He became one of the most celebrated and politically influential Urdu writers of his time. The Pakistan authorities feared his power and in 1951 arrested and sentenced him to four years in prison. Faiz subsequently served two other prison sentences.

Firsthand experience inspired Faiz's 'A Prison Daybreak', which is as powerful as Oscar Wilde's 'Ballad of Reading Gaol' in its message—the serenity of sleep and dreaming, the nightmare of waking to another day of humiliation, pain, and restriction.

Night wasn't over
when the moon stood beside my bed

and said, "You've drunk your sleep to the dregs,
your share of that wine is finished for this night."

My eyes tore themselves from a dream of passion—
they said farewell to my lover's image, still
lingering in the night's stagnant waters
that were spread, like a sheet, over the earth.
Silver whirlpools began their dervish dance
as lotuses of stars fell from the moon's hands.
Some sank. Some rose to the surface,
floated, and opened their petals.
Night and daybreak had fallen desperately
into each other's arms.

In the courtyard,
the prisoners emerged slowly
from a backdrop of gloom. They were shining,
for the dew of sleep had washed, for that moment,
all grief for their country from their eyes,
all agony of separation from their lovers.

But there's a drum, far off. A siren wails.
The furnished guards, their faces pale,
begin their reluctant rounds, in step
with stifled screams from torture rooms.
The cries of those who'll be broken on the rack awake
just as light breezes intoxicated with sleep awake.
Poison awakes. Nothing in the world is asleep.
A door opens in the distance, another is shut.
A chain rasps, then shrieks.
A knife opens a lock's heart, far off,

and a window begins to break its head,
like a madman, against the wind.

So it is the enemies of life awake
and crush the delicate spirit
that keeps me company in my barren despair
while the prisoners and I wait, all day and night,
for a rebel prince of legends to come
with burning arrows, ready to pierce
these tyrant hearts of stone and steel.

Death of a Financier

STEVIE SMITH (1902–1971)

Selected by Jeremy

Stevie Smith wrote both poetry and novels; she had an amazing wit and astutely observed the world. Her first book, *Novel on Yellow Paper,* was published in 1936. A year later she published her first poetry book, *A Good Time Was Had by All*.

Her prodigious poetry coincided with a new media age when, in the 1950s, she did many recordings and broadcasts of her poems. Glenda Jackson starred as Smith in a film (*Stevie*, 1978) about her life.

My mother liked Smith and introduced me to her poetry. Smith's many wonderful poems make it difficult to choose just one. In 'A Soldier Dear to Us', Smith describes, in an obliquely humorous way, the plight of soldiers coming home from the First World War, the traumas they suffered but never felt able to talk about, and how she tried to understand what they were going through as a child.

'Death of a Financier' raises profound questions in its few lines. At the end of their lives everyone looks back on their actions. Here Smith imagines a financier fearing God's wrath after a career based on greed.

Deal not with me God as I have dealt with Man
In the prosperity which thou hast given me
Helpless in his need a careless course I ran
And now oh Lord that thou hast driven me
To my last gasp, I pray for all I am not worth
Deal not with me as I have dealt on earth.

You Are (To My Sons)
ANTONIO GUERRERO RODRÍGUEZ (1958–)
Selected by Len

Antonio Guerrero Rodríguez was one of the Cuban Five (also known as the Miami Five) who were arrested in 1998 on false charges of espionage. The five men were incarcerated without visitation rights for over ten years. It was one of the worst miscarriages of justice in U.S. legal history.

Many hundreds of famous individuals, along with dozens of legal organisations, protested and joined the campaign to have them released. I was deeply involved in the campaign and solicited the support of the American trade unions and, of course, the British and Irish Labour movement.

At the 2008 TUC Conference, I made a speech highlighting the plight of 'the Five.' I described a TV interview with the wife of Gerardo Hernández Nordelo (another of the Five), Adriana Pérez, in which she was asked what she had found most difficult since her husband's incarceration. She responded: 'Every morning, when I look around my empty kitchen table, where I had always dreamt and hoped my children would be.' It was heartrending. Then I read Rodríguez's poem aloud. There wasn't a dry eye in the house.

Some years later, on December 17, 2014, I was in a meeting at my office when my secretary interrupted to tell me that Leo Gerard—president of United Steelworkers (USW), a friend, and an ally who had been trying to persuade President Obama to release the Five—was on the phone. 'Lennie, they are in the air, the Cubans are going home,' he said. This was a great example of international solidarity.

Pérez and Nordelo have since had three children. The kitchen table is full, and dreams have come true.

Here is the poem that brought tears to hard-nosed British trade unionists' eyes.

∼

You are my hand
If I cannot greet faraway friends,
You are my voice
If I cannot denounce in the round table of ideas,
You are my smile
If I cannot console in the purest hour,
You are my dream
If the moment arrives that I cannot dream.

∼

Der fremder in der fremd

IRENA KLEPFISZ (1941–)

Selected by Jeremy

Irena Klepfisz was born in Warsaw, Poland. Her father and mother were both active in the Bund, a workers' organisation in the Jewish community. Klepfisz's father was killed on the second day of the Warsaw Ghetto uprising in 1943. A couple of months before his death, he managed to smuggle Klepfisz and her mother out of the ghetto. Klepfisz was placed in an orphanage while her mother worked as a maid. Later, the two fled to the Polish countryside, where, with the help of local peasant communities, they hid from the Nazis and survived until the liberation of Poland in 1944. After the war, Klepfisz and her mother went to Sweden and a few years later, when Klepfisz was eight years old, they emigrated to the U.S.

Klepfisz is an activist in every sense of the word. She has spent her life dedicated to workers' movements. She founded the Jewish Women's Committee to end the occupation of the West Bank and Gaza and was also part of Di Vilde Chayes (the Wild Beasts), a Jewish feminist group. Having grown up all over the world, Klepfisz has said that there is no language in which she is completely rooted.

Her writings and expression as a feminist and lesbian are rightly well respected and her activism undimmed. 'Der fremder in der fremd' is complex, deeply moving, and full of historical understanding and empathy.

Gedenkst? Do you remember
when you were a stranger among strangers

a fremder on papirn a stranger without papers?

Gedenkst di frages? those endless questions

Ver zayt ir? Fun vanen kumt ir?
who are you? where are you from?
why are you here and not there?

ver zaynen geven ayere shkheynim?
who were your neighbors? where was the school?
what work did you do? what can you do here
that you couldn't do there?

Nokh amol for the third fourth fifth time
Ver zayt ir? Fun vanen kumt ir?
who are you? where are you from?
why are you here and not there?

Ver iz der man? ver iz di froy?
who is this man? who is this woman?
Un di papirn? and their papers?

un dos kind? and this child?
did you find it here? or bring it from there?
do you have a passport? for him? for her?
farn kind that one with the dark hair?

Nokh amol for the tenth eleventh twelfth time
Ver zayt ir? Fun vanen kumt ir?
who are you? where are you from?
why are you here and not there?

who do you know here? who did you know there?
where will you sleep here? how did you sleep there?

un ayere khaloymes:
what do you dream of here? what did you dream of there?
where will you work here? what work did you do there?
and why can't you just work there?

vu iz di vize di grine karte der pasport
visa? green card? passport? photo? from here and from there?

and why did you cut your hair?

un dos kind? and why did you bring
this child here and not leave it there?

Nokh amol for the eighteenth nineteenth twentieth time
ver zayt ir? Fun vanen kumt ir?
farvos zayt ir do? un nisht geblibn dortn?
why are you here? and why didn't you just stay there?

∽

Greetings to the People of Europe!

ALEMU TEBEJE

Selected by Jeremy

The media endlessly talks about 'invasions of migrants' with no context, and our government has passed the most draconian legislation to limit refugee arrivals from anywhere outside Europe. Far from finding the welcoming continent Europe often claims to be, any desperate person fleeing from war-torn places to Europe will face barbed wire, searchlights, and internment camps.

I have visited refugee camps in many parts of the world and witnessed the innovation and desperation of people looking for safety and an opportunity to thrive. The Jungle, an infamous refugee camp in Calais, France, has become synonymous with desperation. I visited The Jungle before it was closed in 2016. It was a traumatic experience, the camp was prone to flooding, and lacking many services. People were living in stress and fear. I visited again, after the camp's closure, and witnessed a town under siege by the police. I saw refugees from every war-torn country who had risked everything to obtain safety in Europe. Nobody risks their lives unless they are desperate, and the ironic and sad reality is that their desperation is often the result of European policies.

Poetry hardly seems a place for desperation, but poems are a means of conveying pain and hardship, prompting future generations to question those in power and demand more. In only eighteen lines, Alemu Tebeje's poem 'Greetings to the People of Europe' succinctly summarises the history of colonialism. Tebeje was born and grew up in Ethiopia and moved to London in the 1990s. He lives near Grenfell Tower, the London social housing complex that burned down in 2017, killing seventy-two people. His perceptive writing gives huge meaning to the tragedy of Grenfell. That same year, American artist Jenny Holzer projected the poem onto public buildings in Denmark, Italy, the U.S., and the U.K.

Over land and sea, your fathers came to Africa
and unpacked bibles by the thousand,
filling our ancestors with words of love:

if someone slaps your right cheek,
　　let him slap your left cheek too!
if someone takes your coat,
　　let him have your trousers too!

now we, their children's children,
inheriting the words your fathers left behind,
our bodies slapped and stripped
by our lifetime presidents,

are braving seas and leaky boats,
cold waves of fear—let salt winds punch
our faces and your coast-guards
pluck us from the water like oily birds!

but here we are at last to knock
at your front door,
hoping against hope that you remember
all the lovely words your fathers preached to ours.

The International
CLIVE BRANSON (1907–1944)

The Volunteer
CECIL DAY LEWIS (1904–1972)

Selected by Len

Throughout history there have been great deeds of bravery—individuals against all odds engaging in a cause that altered the course of events. It's important that such heroism is recorded so it can be remembered in a way that inspires.

In 1936, Francisco Franco and his fascist followers started a Civil War in an effort to overthrow the democratically elected Republican government in Spain. Up against powerful forces, the Republicans fought to defend democracy. Thousands of likeminded comrades came from different countries to help, including from the UK and Ireland. They formed the International Brigade. These people had great courage and many lost their lives. One of my heroes from this time is Jack Jones, a docker in Garston (Liverpool). At twenty-five, he travelled over the Pyrenees to join the fight and was shot and injured in the famous battle of Ebro.

Christy Moore, the renowned Irish singer, wrote the song 'Viva La Quinta Brigada' to commemorate the Irishmen who joined the International Brigade. His song also depicts the Irishmen (Blueshirts) who were encouraged by the Catholic Church to go to Spain to fight for Franco, a shameful act by the Church against democracy. The International Brigade Memorial Trust (IBMT) works to keep alive the memory of those who fought for democracy. When I was the Unite general secretary, I had the privilege of speaking at IBMT's annual event in London. At a rally in London marking the return of the International Brigade they were met with a large banner featuring a quote from Lord Byron:

> 'Yet freedom! yet thy banner, torn but fraying
> Streams like the thunderstorm against the wind.'

My son Ian recently gave me a book of poems from Spain. Most of the poems are written by relatively unknown combatants. Clive Branson was one such man, an artist and poet in his own right, who was imprisoned during the War and sadly later died in World War II in 1944.

We'd left our training base
And by the time night fell
Stood facing the Universe
Singing 'The International'.

I remember it so well
Waiting in the station yard
The darkness stood around still
And the stars, masses, stared.

That's when I first understood
One is never alone in this fight.
I'd thought the 'goodbye' was for good
And left *all* behind that night.

But everything new that I meet
No matter how strange and uncertain,
Holds something familiar that
Proves the fight is still on.

How often I've marched, and marching
I sang of an England unseen,
Watched the great crowds gathering
And the tramp of their feet beat in tune.

Even in the grip of prison
I joined in the singing of millions
As they wait at their wayside station
That leads to the battle lines.

I'm singing in every country
Where I tread through the streets of Time,
One man, one woman, humanity,
The 'International' our theme.

∽

C. Day Lewis, who became the poet laureate in 1968, expressed the voice of liberty in his poetry about the Spanish Civil War.

∽

Tell them in England, if they ask
What brought us to these wars,
To this plateau beneath the night's
Grave manifold of stars—

It was not fraud or foolishness,
Glory, revenge, or pay:
We came because our open eyes
Could see no other way.

There was no other way to keep
Man's flickering truth alight:
These stars will witness that our course
Burned briefer, not less bright.

Beyond the wasted olive-groves,
The furthest lift of land,
There calls a country that was ours
And here shall be regained.

Shine on us, memoried and real,
Green-water-silken meads:
Rivers of home, refresh our path
Whom here your influence leads.

Here in a parched and stranger place
We fight for England free,
The good our fathers won for her,
The land they hoped to see.

The Jumper

CAROLINE SMITH

Selected by Len

Immigration has always made headline news. My family's roots go back to Ireland, when many millions were forced to flee because of the famine brought about by British neglect at best, and a deliberate act of genocide at worst. Irish people were subjected to the same type of bigotry and attacks that other migrants suffer today.

Throughout history, the ruling elite have used groups of people to divide the working class—they spread lies, smears, and innuendos to hide their own failure to govern fairly and to protect their privilege, position, and wealth. The hate that the ruling elite and their newspaper mouthpieces peddle is despicable. Ruling elites deliberately play on fear, and the dog-whistle rhetoric of politicians helps fan the flames, playing into the hands of the far right. From time to time, neofascists will emerge from the ruling elites' stories.

Black people brought over from the Caribbean in the 1940s and '50s (the so-called Windrush generation) to assist and build the British economy were attacked and vilified. The Tory government has denied them the rights of citizenship and spread vile racist lies that make people of color the scapegoats for society's ills.

I have fought against racism all my life. I believe it is evil to attempt to blame and persecute individuals who are deemed to be 'different'—they are not; they have the same problems and aspirations as everyone else.

Of course, it is important to understand the concerns of people. You cannot leave a vacuum that will be filled by the far right. Myths and lies need to be challenged and explained for what they are. There are times when I am dismayed by how gullible people can be. Do they forget when racism ruled much of Europe in the 1930s, resulting in the unbelievable horrors of the Holocaust? Neofascism is once again raising its head throughout the continent and we must all be vigilant.

You won't be surprised to know that, for me, the answer to these issues lies in politics. However, I also have a simpler way of looking at things. What would I do if my family was suffering and our lives seemed endlessly intolerable? I would do anything to seek something better.

Most of those who come to our shores are decent, frightened human beings, and our compassion should dictate our response.

Caroline Smith's *The Immigration Handbook* was given to me by my friend Barry Gardiner M.P. Shortlisted for the 2016 Ted Hughes Award, it is a moving record of the global movement of people, the story of our time. Drawing on her experience as an immigration caseworker in London, Smith's poems brought tears to my eyes. I have chosen one of them here.

She remembered those first weeks
training as a nurse in a foreign land –
homesick, cold.
How she missed her family.
How she had been tempted:
all the colours,
beautiful designs
and how she'd slipped one into her bag.

How she'd been caught,
but thought the Judge had been kind.

How her family had come to join her —
their excitement,
their first days at school.
How they flourished.
How she never told them.
How she'd forgotten
until now, when the letter came
refusing them all
because of her criminal act.
How she couldn't explain to her children.
How she could see no other way —
how without her, they'd be allowed
to stay.

With A Little Help from Our Friends . . .

Strange Fruit

ABEL MEEROPOL (1903–1986)

Selected by Karie Murphy

'Strange Fruit' is an anti-lynching poem by Abel Meeropol. In 1930, Meeropol came across a photograph that captured the lynching of two Black men in Indiana. The horrifying image haunted him for days and prompted him to put pen to paper. 'Strange Fruit' was published in 1937 and later set to music.

In 1939, Billie Holiday famously sang 'Strange Fruit' at Café Society in New York's Greenwich Village. A twenty-three-year-old Holiday walked up to the mic for her final song of the night. Per her request, the waiters stopped serving and the room went completely dark, save for a spotlight on her face. She sang softly, in her raw and emotional voice.

I first heard the song at a union conference in Dundee in 1999, in the same year *Time* magazine designated 'Strange Fruit' the song of the century. It is equally as powerful when read in its original form, and leaves one unable to forget the bitter truth of a nation plagued with racism.

On a recent trip to Memphis, the lyrics echoed in my mind, having arrived in the same week that Tyre Nichols lost his life at the hands of local police officers. In New Orleans a few days later, I felt a chill when the song was performed by Kandace Springs, a young artist and campaigner for the Black Lives Matter movement.

When reading it, I feel both simmering rage and profound sadness about what was happening during the time when Meeropol wrote his poem. Society has yet again been galvanised into campaigning for equality and civil rights both in the U.S. and around the world. The poem remains as relevant today as it was when written ninety years ago.

∼

Southern trees bear a strange fruit,
    (Blood on the leaves and blood at the root,)
Black body swinging in the southern breeze,
    Strange fruit hanging from the poplar trees.

Pastoral scene of the gallant South
    (The bulging eyes and the twisted mouth,)
Scent of magnolia, sweet and fresh,
    (And the sudden smell of burning flesh.)

Here is a fruit for the crows to pluck,
    For the rain to gather, for the wind to suck,
For the sun to rot, for a tree to drop,
    Here is a strange and bitter crop.

∼

Say not the Struggle Nought Availeth

ARTHUR HUGH CLOUGH (1819–1861)

Selected by Ken Loach

Poetry can spring from anger, outrage, compassion, and a fierce determination to stand with the oppressed. In rereading some of the poems that have stayed with me, I am struck by the passion and energy that can lift our spirits and strengthen our resolve.

It was hard to choose just one poem amongst so many. The great socialist poet and dramatist Bertolt Brecht was prolific; 'A Worker Reads History' is one of my favourite of his poems. It asks why it is kings and emperors who win battles and build palaces:

> Was it the kings who hauled the craggy blocks of stone?
> And Babylon, so many times destroyed.
> Who built the city up each time? In which of Lima's houses,
> That city glittering with gold, lived those who built it?

Christopher Logue, activist and poet, wrote 'Know Thy Enemy'. It begins:

> he does not care what colour you are
> provided you work for him

And ends:

> Sooner than lose the things he owns
> he will destroy the world.

These lines could not be more prescient given the current environmental disasters caused by the exploitation of the world's resources.

How far back in time should we go? John Ball's couplet from the 'Peasants' Revolt', in 1381, still resonates:

> When Adam delved and Eve span
> Who was then the Gentleman?

William Morris, who should be as well-known for his socialism as for his wallpaper designs, made a similar point, five centuries later:

> No man is good enough to be another's master.

The great works of Percy Bysshe Shelley, such as his poems after the Peterloo massacre, are well-known and inspirational. His short poem 'Men of England' is as precise a demand for revolutionary change as we could imagine. First the questions:

> Men of England, wherefore plough
> For the Lords who lay ye low?

Then the demands:

> Sow seed—but let no tyrant reap:
> Find wealth—let no imposter heap:
> Weave robes—let not the idle wear:
> Forge arms—in your defence to bear.

William Blake has a striking image to describe what we call false consciousness. It is the idea, which is convenient for the ruling class and perpetuated by their propagandists, that inequality and exploitation are natural to the human condition. 'The poor are always with us', elites say, with a resigned shrug of their shoulders. Their concept of freedom includes the free market and the right to profit from another's labour. Blake summarises it in his poem 'London'. After describing the desperation he sees around him, he writes:

> In every cry of every Man,
> In every Infant's cry of fear,
> In every voice: in every ban,
> The mind-forg'd manacles I hear

Our task is to unlock the manacles that blind us to the reality of how the world works to deny us social justice, security, and peace. It was my friend and comrade Paul Laverty who shared Blake's words with me.

More old favourites from childhood demand a mention. 'The Vicar of Bray' is a song from the eighteenth century about a cleric who changed his principles to suit those in power. There are plenty of MPs on the Labour benches of Parliament who do that today.

And here is Hilaire Belloc's 'Justice of the Peace', which addresses a poor man or woman brought before him about the rights of property:

> You have a shirt, a brimless hat, a shoe
> And half a coat. I am the Lord benign
> Of fifty hundred acres of fat land
> To which I have a right. You understand?

The Tory MPs of vast wealth lecture us on public morality and tell us they will end the poverty that their system produces.

The poem I would like to include in this anthology does not match Shelley, Blake, or Donne, but it does speak to us when, as so often happens, the struggle we wage seems hopeless and the odds against us overwhelming. We sense our power, only to see the power of the state used to defeat us.

We have seen the 1945 settlement of the welfare state dismantled; the great miners' strike of 1984 betrayed; the people who marched in their millions against Tony Blair's war on Iraq discounted, and that illegal, disastrous war fought in our name. Defeat breeds pessimism and destroys confidence. This pessimism only intensifies when Labour leaders put the interests of the powerful before the masses whom they are elected to represent. In these times it is particularly important for us to remember our strength—the exploiters need the exploited to create their wealth. The working class has the power, and the urgent need, to end the injustice, poverty, and environmental destruction we now face.

Here is a short poem by the Victorian Arthur Hugh Clough. It was written after the failure of Chartism in 1848, but it may refer to a battle fought in Italy. It is a stirring call to continue to fight, however faint the prospect of victory. We might not see the whole picture, the enemy may be weaker than we think, and other allies may join us. Victory, for us, means a sustainable world of peace, universal human rights, and social and economic justice, where, to quote Ball again, all things be held in common. In our minds' eye, we can see this world on the horizon; it is still a possibility. Believe it!

Say not the struggle nought availeth,
    The labour and the wounds are vain,
The enemy faints not, nor faileth,
    And as things have been they remain.

If hopes were dupes, fears may be liars;
    It may be, in yon smoke concealed,
Your comrades chase e'en now the fliers,
    And, but for you, possess the field.

For while the tired waves, vainly breaking
    Seem here no painful inch to gain,
Far back through creeks and inlets making,
    Comes silent, flooding in, the main.

And not by eastern windows only,
    When daylight comes, comes in the light,
In front the sun climbs slow, how slowly,
    But westward, look, the land is bright.

From Moss Side: For Morris

CARLA HENRY

Selected by Maxine Peake

'From Moss Side' is one of my favourite pieces of poetry because it depicts the powerful effects of activism and solidarity through generations.

Carla Henry wrote this poem only weeks after learning about the activist Olive Elaine Morris. Jamaican-born, Morris was a leader in the squatters' rights movement of the 1970s. She was a Black nationalist and a feminist who became a key organiser in the Black Women's Movement in the UK and co-founder of the Brixton Black Women's Group and the Organisation of Women of African and Asian Descent in London. When she was seventeen years old, she accused officers of the Metropolitan police force of assaulting her after she had intervened to prevent the beating of a Nigerian diplomat in Brixton, South London. She later became a communist and joined the British Black Panthers. She died from non-Hodgkin's lymphoma in 1979, at the age of just twenty-seven. Alongside her friends and comrades, her life and work have been commemorated by the Remembering Olive Collective.

Henry saw many similarities between Morris's life and her own, an emotional recognition that one can feel tumbling out of the page. As all great activist poetry does, the poem connects our present day to the very personal story of a young Mancunian Black woman navigating the here and now: It holds a mirror up to society and honors Morris's legacy.

Jheeeeeeeze. Olive Morris
What would you say bout Boris
Wid him chat bout victimisation
How him a try fi part/fi we nation

27 years
Too short
Olive Elaine Morris
You brought/with you
From Jamaica/St Cathrine
Age nine
Da fire fee expose da bloodclart swine

Who still to dis day a put dem knee pon
We neck

Try tek way fi we speech
Try keep we fi dem pet
Den when we raise/dem want fi call we fret

Dem arrest you fi stepping out of ya lane

Fi try save a diplomat brother/dem beat ya all de same

"That's the right colour for your body," they said
Though they left you with bruises

Cha!

Still Morris refuses/to shut up di mowht
To hold back di fire

Fi Morris she only did lift we up higher

When da paraffin heater did left we fi dead
March/Morris/March to da housing instead

Left people Pitney/fi da housing fi look after
Told dem
Change tings/we nar teck dem home/to disaster
She made tings happen
Show we how fi run da show
Come from London to Manchester/Moss Side/to blow

Jhezzze Olive Morise set up committe and co op
A black Panther movement/a dat how she grow up

Left school before qualifications give out
A economics and social science degree
A dat she about
Left us her legacy in 1952
Olive Elaine Morris/
We
Pour
Libation
Fi
You

Even though they didn't chose/your face fi de pound
Thank you for helping us stand/on this here ground

You were born in St Cathrine just like fi me daddy
Died of the same cancer dat trie to take me Mammy

Olive/Elaine/Morris/
Fi da homeless
Fi da women
Fi da black power you stood
For your sake and sacrifice/
Olive/Morris

WE come good

Like a Life-Giving Sun

HAFIZ (1325–1390)

Selected by Rob Delaney

I have chosen this poem because it clearly illustrates both how difficult life in this world is *and* the fact that there is a way through it. I found this poem when I was in my twenties and starting to accept that we can and will get torn apart by all kinds of forces, external and internal, and that while love can help us through, it takes discipline to access and receive it.

We cannot 'coast' through life; we must work hard and correct course as needed. That's not 'bad'; it's just how it is! So to me, this poem is real as hell, beautiful, and short enough to memorise and share with others!

Hafiz was a poet whose work is seen as a pinnacle of Persian literature by ordinary Iranians. Many keep collections of his poetry in their homes, and memorize lines from it to use as everyday proverbs. My favourite words of his are: 'Love is simply creation's greatest joy'.

You could become a great horseman
And help to free yourself and this world
Though only if you and prayer become Sweet Lovers.

It is a naive man who thinks we are not
Engaged in a fierce battle,
For I see and hear brave foot soldiers
All around me going mad,
Falling on the ground in excruciating pain.

You could become a victorious horseman
And carry your heart through this world
Like a life-giving sun
Though only if you and God become
Sweet Lovers.

The Peat Bog Soldiers

JOHANN ESSER (1896–1971) and WOLFGANG LANGHOFF (1901–1966)

Selected by Michael Rosen

My Father used to sing 'The Peat Bog Soldiers'. The song was written by prisoners in Nazi moorland labour camps in Lower Saxony, Germany. In one camp, the socialist and communist internees who were banned from singing existing political songs, wrote and composed their own. A miner, Johann Esser, and an actor, Wolfgang Langhoff, wrote the words, and the music was composed by Rudi Goguel. It was later adapted by Hanns Eisler and Ernst Busch.

My parents' view of Germany and the Nazis didn't align with the narrative in postwar Britain when I was growing up. For example, there was a blanket condemnation of Germany and all Germans. Because my parents were communists (until 1957), their view was that the Nazis began their war-loving, genocidal regime to wipe out communists, socialists, and trade unionists in Germany. The story of 1933–1939 is one of accommodation, appeasement, and collaboration with the Nazi government.

The song has a particular appeal to me because it was mostly written by those being persecuted—the song itself is an act of resistance.

∼

Any directions you might see,
Bog and heath is everywhere.
Here are no birds to sing for me
The oaks, they stand twisted and bare.

We are the bog battalion,
On spade instead of stallion,
In bog.

In such a deserted landscape
Just for us, this compound dire.
Far from friends and with no escape
We are cached behind barbed wire.

We are the bog battalion,
On spade instead of stallion,
In bog.

Columns long, we head for the bog
To dig the early morning.
We sweat in sun, work like a dog,
And think of loved ones mourning.

We are the bog battalion,
On spade instead of stallion,
In bog.

Thought to home and hearth do return,
To parents, wife and children.
Many a breast may sigh and yearn
To leave this prison, when, oh when?

We are the bog battalion,
On spade instead of stallion,
In bog.

The patrols guard us day and night,
Escape is a losing sport.
Your life's not worth attempted flight,
Four rings of wire fence the fort.

We are the bog battalion,
On spade instead of stallion,
In bog.

Complaining will not set us free;
Winter can't last forever.
The time will come when we will see,
Our homeland ours, together.

Then no more bog battalion
No spade instead of stallion
In bog.

Peterloo: Estimated Wrap 19.30

KATE RUTTER

Selected by Julie Hesmondhalgh

In 2017 I had the extraordinary privilege of being a small part of Mike Leigh's epic film about the Peterloo massacre. Along with a massive cast of mainly northern actors, including the peerless Maxine Peake, I spent months immersing myself in the story of struggle, courage, and state violence during this vital and tragic moment in working-class history.

During the long process of rehearsing and filming, I made friends for life, and the seven of us who proudly represented the Manchester Female Reformers in the film have continued to lift each other up daily, sharing sisterly solidarity and political outrage on our dedicated WhatsApp group, aptly named Liberty or Death!

Kate Rutter, a wonderful poet as well as a brilliant actor and tireless activist, wrote and published this poem about her deeply felt connection with the women of 1819, whose stories we were entrusted to tell, and how we continue to be inspired by their bravery.

It is included here with Rutter's permission, and in recognition of the contribution of women, including our sisters from the global majority, LGBTQ+ and disabled communities, in working-class struggle, then and now.

∽

We were woken and called into the light and what a light it was.
Lamps concealed in crevices were shone through sheets of Sunday white.
Everywhere the bellows moved, fog poured like weavers' winter breath.

Many hands, all dressed like men, made ready and when our living
    likeness
stepped into the room, and what a room it was, high and clear of cot-
    ton dust,
we heard again the words that were to cut us down. Over and over
those words were spoke but not to beat us with, this was no courtroom.
The likenesses had a well-fed look and clean. They sat on ample backsides
and with hands like children's hands on laps, at last they understood.

Was it our place to warn them then, to break the years and show our-
    selves?
Or were we fetched back only for witness? We breathed hunger in
    their ears.
We wove flowers and laurel leaves. We marched the square in step
    with them.

And when the horsemen rode with sabres raised, we grieved our
    opened breasts,
our slashed and ruined faces. Although the square was not our square,
    the time
was not our time, on that day it was all such squares, littered with shoes
    and roses.

Please Call Me by My True Names

THICH NHAT HANH (1926–2022)

Selected by Francesca Martinez

Buddhist monk Thich Nhat Hanh is an inspirational figure. Despite living through decades of war in Vietnam and nearly forty years in exile, he never wavered in his commitment to spreading peace and compassion. As he carried out his lifelong mission to reduce suffering and inspire joy by promoting his vision of 'engaged Buddhism', he not only demonstrated that it is possible to simultaneously walk the path of the political activist and the spiritual teacher, he also showed that ultimately they are the same path.

Thay, as he was known by his many students, was a wonderful writer and a beautiful poet. He responded to the death and devastation that plagued his home country with words of tenderness and insight. His many writings, in more than a hundred books, invite us to look more deeply at ourselves and the difficult situations we face. As he experienced firsthand, in the face of injustice, waves of pain, anger, and hatred often arise. Thay saw that these emotions are powerful fuel for political engagement but warned that they are also corrupting—that they blind us to important truths, often leading to interventions that produce further suffering. He taught the importance of neither ignoring nor acting on these feelings, but instead learning how to transform them. The best fuel for action, he advised, is always compassion.

It was Thay's principled and influential call for peace (he was nominated for the Nobel Peace Prize by Martin Luther King Jr) that led to both North and South Vietnam denying him the right to return home after campaigning abroad. His refusal to support either side in the Vietnam War, 'The War of American Aggression' as it is known in Vietnam, left him and his followers isolated and at risk of violence. Students and friends of his were imprisoned or killed for their social work and peace campaigning. Unable to return to Vietnam, he continued to work for peace while helping to organise material support for thousands of desperate Vietnamese. The School of Youth for Social Service that he founded in Vietnam—a grassroots organisation based on the principles of nonviolence—attracted over ten thousand volunteers.

As the war came to an end, many Vietnamese fled their devastated homeland by boat, seeking refuge in countries across Southeast Asia. Estimates suggest half of them died in the ocean before arriving at their destination. Those who did reach their destination were often pushed back out to sea by hostile governments unwilling to provide sanctuary. Throughout these perilous voyages, those seeking refuge faced the added danger of attacks from pirates. It was hearing news of one such attack that led to the writing of my chosen poem, 'Please Call Me by My True Names'.

The news arrived by letter: A twelve-year-old girl had drowned herself in the ocean after being raped by a Thai pirate. Intense feelings of anger rose in Thay. His response was to enter a long meditation—on the girl, on the pirate, and on himself—after which he wrote what became one of his most famous poems. He later explained: 'In my meditation, I saw that if I had been born in the village of the pirate and raised in the same conditions as he was, I would now be the pirate . . .'

Thay's words, here and in the poem, are a reminder that every person and every choice emerges from a set of conditions. When conditions produce ignorance, pain, greed, anger, or hopelessness, those who are impacted are likely to create further suffering for others and themselves. Thay points out that we all have the seeds of hatred, greed, and ignorance in us, just as we all have the seeds of compassion, love, and understanding. What matters is which seeds are watered by our life experience and which seeds we water in others.

I believe Thay is right: Under different conditions, he could have become a violent pirate, and perhaps the pirate who destroyed the young girl's life could have become a peace-loving monk. This understanding is essential if we are to respond to society's problems.

War will never end war. Violence will never end violence. Hate will never end hate. To end these things, we need to change the conditions that breed them, while cultivating their opposites in ourselves and the world. It is a difficult lesson, but in our increasingly polarised society I believe it is one we must learn. As Thay liked to say: 'There is no way to peace, peace is the way.'

'Please Call Me by My True Names' has inspired me deeply. Whenever anger erupts, I want to try and look deeper into the situation that sparked it, and to keep looking until I find a way to reconnect with compassion and love. I hope his words touch you as they did me.

Don't say that I will depart tomorrow—
even today I am still arriving.

Look deeply: every second I am arriving
to be a bud on a Spring branch,
to be a tiny bird, with still-fragile wings,
learning to sing in my new nest,
to be a caterpillar in the heart of a flower,

to be a jewel hiding itself in a stone.

I still arrive, in order to laugh and to cry,
to fear and to hope.
The rhythm of my heart is the birth and death
of all that is alive.

I am a mayfly metamorphosing
on the surface of the river.
And I am the bird
that swoops down to swallow the mayfly.

I am a frog swimming happily
in the clear water of a pond.
And I am the grass-snake
that silently feeds itself on the frog.

I am the child in Uganda, all skin and bones,
my legs as thin as bamboo sticks.
And I am the arms merchant,
selling deadly weapons to Uganda.

I am the twelve-year-old girl,
refugee on a small boat,
who throws herself into the ocean
after being raped by a sea pirate.

And I am also the pirate,
my heart not yet capable
of seeing and loving.

I am a member of the politburo,
with plenty of power in my hands.

And I am the man who has to pay
his "debt of blood" to my people
dying slowly in a forced-labor camp.

My joy is like Spring, so warm
it makes flowers bloom all over the Earth.
My pain is like a river of tears,
so vast it fills the four oceans.

Please call me by my true names,
so I can hear all my cries and laughter at once,
so I can see that my joy and pain are one.

Please call me by my true names,
so I can wake up
and the door of my heart
could be left open,
the door of compassion.

The Horses

EDWIN MUIR (1887–1959)

Selected by Alexei Sayle

'The Horses' is a powerful and moving poem highly relevant to our current politically charged times. It is set in a period following some kind of war that has destroyed human civilisation. A new and better way to rebuild society post-catastrophe is suggested by the return of the horses and the forging of a kinder, more respectful alliance between mankind and animals. There is something about it that always makes me cry.

Barely a twelvemonth after
The seven days war that put the world to sleep,
Late in the evening the strange horses came.
By then we had made our covenant with silence,
But in the first few days it was so still
We listened to our breathing and were afraid.
On the second day
The radios failed; we turned the knobs; no answer.
On the third day a warship passed us, heading north,
Dead bodies piled on the deck. On the sixth day
A plane plunged over us into the sea. Thereafter

Nothing. The radios dumb;
And still they stand in corners of our kitchens,
And stand, perhaps, turned on, in a million rooms
All over the world. But now if they should speak,
If on a sudden they should speak again,
If on the stroke of noon a voice should speak,
We would not listen, we would not let it bring
That old bad world that swallowed its children quick
At one great gulp. We would not have it again.
Sometimes we think of the nations lying asleep,
Curled blindly in impenetrable sorrow,
And then the thought confounds us with its strangeness.
The tractors lie about our fields; at evening
They look like dank sea-monsters crouched and waiting.
We leave them where they are and let them rust:
"They'll molder away and be like other loam."
We make our oxen drag our rusty plows,
Long laid aside. We have gone back
Far past our fathers' land.
                            And then, that evening
Late in the summer the strange horses came.
We heard a distant tapping on the road,
A deepening drumming; it stopped, went on again
And at the corner changed to hollow thunder.
We saw the heads
Like a wild wave charging and were afraid.
We had sold our horses in our fathers' time
To buy new tractors. Now they were strange to us
As fabulous steeds set on an ancient shield.
Or illustrations in a book of knights.

We did not dare go near them. Yet they waited,
Stubborn and shy, as if they had been sent
By an old command to find our whereabouts
And that long-lost archaic companionship.
In the first moment we had never a thought
That they were creatures to be owned and used.
Among them were some half a dozen colts
Dropped in some wilderness of the broken world,
Yet new as if they had come from their own Eden.
Since then they have pulled our plows and borne our loads
But that free servitude still can pierce our hearts.
Our life is changed; their coming our beginning.

More Time

LINTON KWESI JOHNSON (1952–)

Selected by Gary Younge

My mother died when she was forty-four. She arrived in England from Barbados in 1962 and trained as a nurse and then, when my dad left her with three children aged six and under, she went into teaching so that she would be on holiday when we were. Throughout that time, she supplemented her income by running a holiday play scheme, teaching Asian women English, teaching numeracy and literacy in the local college, or helping run a youth club.

On my office wall I have a photograph of her, the existence of which I only learned about almost twenty years after she died. It was taken by one of her former colleagues at a supplementary school where she worked. She's lying on a sofa, a book laid open in her lap, in what looks like a shallow sleep. As formidable and dynamic a presence as she was, this is one of the images I remember most. I was nineteen when she passed: The lesson that life was both short and precarious was learned relatively young.

The notion that we need more time, the persistent refrain in Linton Kwesi Johnson's poem, speaks very directly to me. And when delivered in Johnson's lyrical style—melodic, playful patois set to a reggae rhythm (the first time I heard 'More Time', he was singing it with a band accompaniment)—it frames a message that both recalls the Caribbean lilt my mother never lost and a comforting cultural cocoon.

Placing joy and relationships at the centre of our understanding of what capitalism takes from us and how resistance to it might be engaged in the most basic human terms is a gift, especially in a moment when the pressure to work more years and longer hours feels relentless.

> *Wi need di shawtah working year*
> *Gi wi di shawtah workin life*
> *More time fi di huzban*
> *More time fi di wife*

Johnson is Black Britain's poet laureate. His long-standing presence in music, poetry, and prose has sat not so much alongside his lifetime of activism around racism, police brutality, and anti-colonial and anti-imperialist struggles as within it. In a 2017 speech accepting an honorary doctorate from South Africa's Rhodes University, he recalls how his literary purpose and trajectory was formulated following an episode of physical police harassment in 1972 in Brixton, when he was just twenty. 'Having heard blues and jazz poetry, I decided that I wanted to write reggae poetry. My verse would be a cultural weapon in the Black liberation struggles.'

More bard than griot, his poetry does not present the Black working class to a white poetry-loving world in exotic, poetic form but to articulate the Black working-class experience in its own vernacular. As such, he speaks truth not about power but to it, finding his capacity to do so from the communities in which he is embedded and which he sees as a source of collective power.

~

Wi mawchin out di ole towards di new centri
Arm wid di new technalagy

Wi gettin more an more producktivity
Some seh tings lookin-up fi prasperity
But if evrywan goin get a share dis time
Ole mentality mus get lef behine

Wi want di shawtah workin day
Gi wi di shawtah workin week
Langah holiday
Wi need decent pay

More time fi leasha
More time fi pleasha
More time fi edificaeshun
More time fi reckreashun
More time fi contemplate
More time fi ruminate
More time
Wi need
More
Time
Gi wi more time

A full time dem abalish unemployment
An revahlushanise laybah deployment
A full time dem banish ovahtime
Mek evrybady get a wok dis time
Wi need a highah quality a livity
Wi need it now an fi evrybady
Wi need di shawtah workin year
Gi wi di shawtah workin life
More time fi di huzban
More time fi di wife
More time fi di children

More time fi wi fren dem
More time fi meditate
More time fi create
More time fi livin
More time fi life
More time
Wi need more time
Gi wi more time

Welling

HANNAH LOWE (1976–)

Selected by Morag Livingstone

This evocative and powerful poem describes the Welling protest that took place in south-east London on October 16, 1993. The protestors were demanding the closure of a British National Party bookshop, a front for the BNP headquarters. The demonstration was held following the murder of Stephen Lawrence and a spate of other racist attacks in the area. The protest attracted sixty thousand anti-racists.

Marking this moment in time, British writer Hannah Lowe starts 'Welling' by describing how the protesters were accused of being 'violent'. We wonder what happened. Those at the front, who witnessed the events, know that it was not the protesters who started the violence. Later in the poem Lowe alludes to this. It is only with the passage of time and uncovering of new evidence that it is confirmed it was the police who turned this peaceful protest into one that injured many.

Lowe takes the reader back in time to the adventure and solidarity pre-demonstration, a time of hope. Details of a 'green cord jacket', 'yellow placards', and a 'beautiful man' reinforce these feelings in the reader. By the middle of the poem, Lowe has lulled us into a false sense of security. We believe all is well. The change in tone comes as a surprise, reflecting the quick turn of events, mirroring a sudden change of atmosphere on that sunny October day of 1993. We feel the terror of a police horse charge. The conclusion is shocking.

In fourteen short lines, Lowe moves us through an emotional rollercoaster of vivid descriptions, the juxtaposition of gentle words and a brutal sense of reality. Vivid mental images form in the mind while reading the poem and stay with you long after. I love this work for its ability to permeate the mind and to raise questions that remain unanswered: Why did this happen?

It's not just a beautifully written poem. It is an important work, not least because Lowe encapsulates how the police in this country responded to anti-racist protesters in 1993. Her writing demonstrates how protesters are vilified and 'othered' when calling for a better society. In the light of recent Black Lives Matter protests and police handling of them, Lowe's poem reminds us of the similarities between 1993 and today. Little appears to have changed. There is still much to do.

On the news that night they called us *violent youth*
but what I remember is the green cord jacket I was wearing
pulled from a bargain bin that morning
and a busload of us singing our way down South,
the yellow placards like a bobbing sea of lollipops,
a beautiful man with dreadlocks, studs in his chin
and us on the frontline, marching and chanting
until the chanting suddenly stopped

then one voice shouted *Police protect the Nazis!*
the police like a wall of giant flies, their graceful white horses,

then silence – no moment in my life do I remember quieter –
before the charges, the bricks, the screams,
two boys with gashed heads running together,
that animal smell, red smoke, blood on my sleeves –

Free Flight

JUNE JORDAN (1936–2002)

Selected by Melissa Benn

I have long admired June Jordan: poet, essayist, teacher, revolutionary activist. Her writing is fiercely political yet still feels colloquial, like having someone quietly talk to you (Jordan herself had a strikingly soft voice) about the most pressing subjects of the day: poverty, rape and sexual violence, racist policing, or the need for solidarity with the world's most marginalised and oppressed. Her essays are a series of vivid chronicles of intersectionality in practice. No one refuses political simplicities more adamantly; she continuously explores the contradictions within and conflict between 'identities', including her own: a Black, bisexual female and a U.S. citizen born of Caribbean immigrants.

In the late 1980s, I got the chance to interview Jordan on stage in London. At the end she read 'Free Flight' with deliberate, joyous, and comic verve. I can still remember the thrill of it. (As well as that soft voice, she had the most fetching and mischievous giggle). The poem is a wonderful jumble of the serious and the playful, capturing how the mind of a tired, wired person works in the small hours. Jordan's thoughts roam from earthquakes to political poets, to Mahler's Ninth Symphony, to the colour of guest towels, to lists of 'light bulbs, lemons, envelopes, ballpoint refills', to her shame at feeling compelled to kiss people she despises at parties 'because the party's like that'. The final lines of 'Free Flight'—'maybe I just need to love myself

myself and / anyway / I'm working on it' —perfectly mimic the drifting of a mind at dawn.

While often describing individual experiences (her own or others), Jordan's writing is always fully (and furiously) alert to the wider forces that shape and press down on any given person, group, or situation. In her essays she writes tenderly of her ten-year marriage to a white political activist with whom she had a son—a marriage more difficult than most, she concludes, in the volatile and racist atmosphere of '50s and '60s America. Or, while enjoying a brief stay at a hotel in the Bahamas, she contemplates the experience of the 'Black Woman described on the card atop my hotel bureau as "Olive the Maid" . . . Olive is older than I am, and I may smoke a cigarette while she changes the sheets on my bed. Whose rights? Whose freedom? Whose desire?' Her account of being caught in the middle of police violence during the funeral of a young Black man in Harlem in the early 1960s is terrifyingly vivid but, half a century later, feels strikingly contemporary. Jordan, it turns out, was not just asking some of the most important questions of her personal and political lifetime but of ours too.

Nothing fills me up at night
I fall asleep for one or two hours then
up again my gut
alarms
I must arise
and wandering into the refrigerator
think about evaporated milk homemade vanilla ice cream
cherry pie hot from the oven with Something Like Vermont
Cheddar Cheese disintegrating luscious
on the top while

mildly
I devour almonds and raisins mixed to mathematical
criteria or celery or my very own sweet and sour snack
composed of brie peanut butter honey and
a minuscule slice of party size salami
on a single whole wheat cracker *no salt added*
Or I read César Vallejo/Gabriela Mistral/last year's
complete anthology or
I might begin another list of things to do
that starts with toilet paper and
I notice that I never jot down fresh
strawberry shortcake: never
even though fresh strawberry shortcake shoots down
raisins and almonds 6 to nothing
effortlessly
effortlessly
is this poem on my list?
light bulbs lemons envelopes ballpoint refill
post office and zucchini
oranges no
it's not
I guess that means I just forgot
walking my dog around the block leads
to a space in my mind where
during the newspaper strike questions
sizzle through suddenly like
Is there an earthquake down in Ecuador?
Did a T.W.A. supersaver flight to San Francisco
land in Philadelphia instead
Or
whatever happened to human rights
in Washington D.C.? Or what about downward destabilization

of the consumer price index
and I was in this school P.S. Tum-Ta-Tum and time came
for me to leave but
No! I couldn't leave: The Rule was anybody leaving
the premises without having taught somebody something
valuable would be henceforth proscribed from the
premises would be forever null and void/dull and
vilified well
I had stood in front of 40 to 50 students running my
mouth and I had been generous with deceitful smiles/soft-
spoken and pseudo-gentle wiles if and when forced
into discourse amongst such adults as constitutes
the regular treacheries of On The Job Behavior
ON THE JOB BEHAVIOR
is this poem on that list
polish shoes file nails coordinate tops and bottoms
lipstick control no
screaming I'm bored because
this is whoring away the hours of god's creation
pay attention to your eyes your hands the twilight
sky in the institutional big windows
no
I did not presume I was not so bold as to put this
poem on that list
then at the end of the class this boy gives me Mahler's 9th
symphony the double album listen
to it let it seep into you he
says transcendental love
he says
I think naw
I been angry all day long/nobody did the assignment
I am not prepared

I am not prepared for so much grace
the catapulting music of surprise that makes me
hideaway my face
nothing fills me up at night
yesterday the houseguest left a brown
towel in the bathroom for tonight
I set out a blue one and
an off-white washcloth seriously
I don't need no houseguest
I don't need no towels/lovers
I just need a dog
Maybe I'm kidding

Maybe I need a woman
a woman be so well you know so wifelike
so more or less motherly so listening so much
the universal skin you love to touch and who the
closer she gets to you the better she looks to me/somebody
say yes and make me laugh and tell me she know she
been there she spit bullets at my enemies she say you
need to sail around Alaska fuck it all try this new
cerebral tea and take a long bath

Maybe I need a man
a man be so well you know so manly so lifelike
so more or less virile so sure so much the deep
voice of opinion and the shoulders like a window
seat and cheeks so closely shaven by a twin-edged
razor blade no oily hair and no dandruff besides/
somebody say yes and make
me laugh and tell me he know he been there he spit
bullets at my enemies he say you need to sail around
Alaska fuck it all and take a long bath

la-ti-dah and lah-ti-dum
what's this socialized obsession with the bathtub

Maybe I just need to love myself myself
(anyhow I'm more familiar with the subject)
Maybe when my cousin tells me you remind me
of a woman past her prime maybe I need
to hustle my cousin into a hammerlock
position make her cry out uncle and
I'm sorry
Maybe when I feel this horrible
inclination to kiss folks I despise
because the party's like that
an occasion to be kissing people
you despise maybe I should tell them kindly
kiss my

Maybe when I wake up in the middle of the night
I should go downstairs
dump the refrigerator contents on the floor
and stand there in the middle of the spilled milk
and the wasted butter spread beneath my dirty feet
writing poems
writing poems
maybe I just need to love myself myself and
anyway
I'm working on it

Warning

JENNY JOSEPH (1932–2018)

Selected by Karie Murphy

This humorous poem was written by a woman who reportedly hated the colour purple!

In our twilight years most of us expect the end of life's pleasures. But in this poem, a woman intent on wearing purple experiences increased pleasure with age, as she no longer needs to consider what others think of her.

Jenny Joseph's poem is a beacon of hope for those sisters who refuse to conform—a love letter written to our future selves. Being on the rebellious side of life isn't easy and rarely occurs without controversy. I fully adopt the 'geri-antics' approach Joseph advocates, much to the embarrassment of my weans.

By the end of the poem, the woman in purple has decided to start living her life in order to have as much fun as possible—disregarding convention, shunning society's rules, and embracing optimism for the future.

The ability to live life as one chooses is a treasure, and being comfortable with oneself is priceless. This sentiment is reflected in both poetry and music—Corrine Bailey Rae's song 'Put Your Records On' is one of the best written examples of a woman learning how to love and accept herself. Joseph's poem speaks in similar terms but goes further, actively encouraging behaviour that has been long discouraged by a society that fails to respect women and a culture that refuses to see beauty in women past a certain age.

'Be who you are and say what you feel, because those who mind don't matter and those who matter don't mind.' 'Warning' is an ode to us non-conformists everywhere.

When I am an old woman I shall wear purple
With a red hat which doesn't go, and doesn't suit me.
And I shall spend my pension on brandy and summer gloves
And satin sandals, and say we've no money for butter.
I shall sit down on the pavement when I'm tired
And gobble up samples in shops and press alarm bells
And run my stick along the public railings
And make up for the sobriety of my youth.
I shall go out in my slippers in the rain
And pick flowers in other people's gardens
And learn to spit.

You can wear terrible shirts and grow more fat
And eat three pounds of sausages at a go
Or only bread and pickle for a week
And hoard pens and pencils and beermats and things in boxes.

But now we must have clothes that keep us dry
And pay our rent and not swear in the street
And set a good example for the children.
We must have friends to dinner and read the papers.

But maybe I ought to practise a little now?
So people who know me are not too shocked and surprised
When suddenly I am old, and start to wear purple.

Calais in Winter

JEREMY CORBYN

This poem was written by Jeremy on a train home after a recent trip to visit the refugee camps in Calais.

Cold wet marshlands surround Calais in winter
Police take tents away from the homeless
The Railway station is protected with razor wire
Motorways have walls on each side
Trees are cut down to create open land
Huge rocks prevent anyone leaving a road

There is fear in Calais
It stalks every official building
It seeps into the minds of the Police
It pervades all thinking
It gives imagination to cold hearted people
To confront the enemy

When they escape to the sea
In flimsy boats at home in a small lake
They have to be stopped
With bayonets puncturing them
Clothing taken that would protect
Against the cold

The enemy comes on foot
In lorries and buses
With few clothes
No money and no food
Few friends
Only memories

Of bombardment and war
Of families in jail
Of crops destroyed
Of empty schools
Of floods and drought
Of bitter travelling

In secret lorries
On mountain paths
In safe houses
Of razor wire
And cameras
Hidden in trees

Volunteers in a big store
Handing clothing and boots
Backpacks and sleeping bags
Gloves and socks
Wood for fires
Medicines too

Huge vats of cooking rice
Aromatic curries
Wholesome bread
Fresh fruit

Clean water in big vats
For the thirsty

Delivered around the town
To enemy groups
Who change location every day
Harrassed by Police
Shunned and abused
By those with a cold heart

Except in one place
A centre in the town
With warmth
And food and power
And for a few hours
To be secure

In the beauty of the sunset
in cold winter time
The setting sun gleams on the Hotel de Ville
A crowd gathers around a white van
To eat what has come
And search for a place to rest

They will be stopped
Thunder politicians
The enemy will not land
Say screaming headlines
They are lawbreakers
Say experts on the radio

Their homes are a long list
Of places near and far

Where wars are fought
And minerals abound
Where money is made
And people disappear

Calais in winter
Is cold and hard
Calais in summer
Is busy and happy
But hot and tense
For the enemy

Contributors

Melissa Benn is a writer, campaigner, lecturer and teacher. She has published nine books, including two novels, *Public Lives* and *One of Us,* which was shortlisted for a British Book Award. Her political writing includes *School Wars: The Battle for Britain's Education* and *Life Lessons: The Case for a National Education Service*. Her journalism and essays have appeared in a wide range of publications, including the *Guardian,* the *New Statesman* and the *Financial Times*. Melissa is a regular public speaker and currently Visiting Professor in Education, Language and Psychology at York St John University.

Rob Delaney is an American comedian, actor, and writer. He is the co-creator and co-star of the Channel 4 comedy *Catastrophe*. Rob is also the author of two books: *A Heart That Works* and *Mother. Wife. Sister. Human. Warrior. Falcon. Yardstick. Turban. Cabbage.*

Julie Hesmondhalgh is an English actor and narrator. She played Hayley Cropper in the ITV soap opera *Coronation Street* between 1998 and 2014. She has also appeared in a range of other television productions including *Cucumber, Happy Valley, Broadchurch* and *The Pact*. Her stage credits include *God Bless the Child* at the Royal Court Theatre in London and *Wit* at the Royal Exchange, Manchester.

Morag Livingstone is a documentary filmmaker, writer, lecturer and internationally published author. She is co-author of two best-selling books: *Hackney Child* and *Tainted Love*. Her latest book, co-written with Matt Foot, *Charged: How the Police Try to Suppress Protest,* exposes the secret imposition of paramilitary policing under Thatcher, and its brutal use against trade unionists, anti-racists, and environmentalists.

Ken Loach is a British film director and screenwriter. His directorial credits include *Cathy Come Home, Days of Hope, Poor Cow, Kes, Land and Freedom, The Wind That Shakes the Barley, I, Daniel Blake, Sorry We Missed You,* and *The Old Oak.* He twice won the Palme d'Or at the Cannes Film Festival, and received a BAFTA for Outstanding British Film.

Francesca Martinez is an English comedian, writer, and actress. She has cerebral palsy but prefers to describe herself as 'wobbly'. She has appeared in the television series *Grange Hill* and *Holby City*. In 2000, Martinez became the first female comic to win the *Daily Telegraph* Open Mic Award at the Edinburgh Festival. She appears regularly on television shows including *Newsnight*, *This Week*, and *Question Time*.

Karie Murphy is a trade unionist and political strategist. She worked as a Health Visitor in Glasgow for 25 years before entering politics. She served as the Chief of Staff to Jeremy Corbyn, Leader of the Opposition, from 2016 to 2020.

Maxine Peake is an English actress and narrator. Her television, film and stage credits include *dinnerladies, Shameless, Silk, The Village, See No*

Evil, *Clubbed*, *Miss Julie*, *Henry IV Parts I and II*, *Hamlet*, *Peterloo*, *Happy Days* and *Talking Heads*. She wrote, directed and starred in the play *Beryl: A Love Story on Two Wheels*.

Michael Rosen is a children's author, poet, presenter, political columnist, broadcaster and activist. He has written 140 books including *We're Going on a Bearhunt*, which was later adapted for stage, a memoir, *So They Call You Pisher!*, and an account of his near-death experience after contracting COVID, *Many Different Kinds of Love: A Story of Life, Death and the NHS*. He served as the UK's Children's Laureate from 2007 to 2009 and won the 2023 PEN Pinter Prize.

Alexei Sayle is a Liverpool-born author, stand-up comedian, television presenter and former recording artist. He was a leading figure in the British alternative comedy movement in the 1980s, a decade in which he released the hit single *Ullo John! Gotta New Motor?* Among his many books is a two-volume autobiography, *Stalin Ate My Homework* and *Thatcher Stole My Trousers*. More recently he has written and appeared in two BBC Radio 4 shows, *Alexei Sayle's Imaginary Sandwich Bar* and *Alexei Sayle's The Absence of Normal*.

Gary Younge is an author, broadcaster, and a professor of sociology at the University of Manchester. He was awarded the 2023 Orwell Prize for Journalism. Formerly a columnist and editor-at-large at the *Guardian*, he is an editorial board member of *The Nation* magazine and Type Media Fellow. He has written for publications including the *New York Review of Books* and the *Financial Times*, and made several radio and television documentaries. His most recent books are *Another Day in the Death of America* and *Dispatches from the Diaspora*.

Jeremy Corbyn is the Member of Parliament for Islington North and was Leader of the Labour Party between 2015 and 2020.

Len McCluskey was, until 2022, the General Secretary of Britain's largest trade union, UNITE. He is the author of the recently published memoir *Always Red*.

Permissions

'In Jerusalem' from *The Butterfly's Burden*, translated by Fady Joudah. © 2007 Mahmoud Darwish. Translation © 2007 Fady Joudah. Reprinted with the permission of The Permissions Company, LLC on behalf of Copper Canyon Press, coppercanyonpress.org.

'I Into History, Now' © 1973 Andrew Salkey. Reprinted with the permission of the Estate of Andrew Salkey.

'The Tree Council' © Mike Jenkins. First published in *Shedding Paper Skin* (Carreg Gwalch), 2015. Reprinted with the permission of the author.

'Do Not Go Gentle Into That Good Night' © The Dylan Thomas Trust, from *The Collected Poems of Dylan Thomas*, published by Weidenfeld & Nicholson. Permission granted by David Higham Associates. (Published in 2014). US and Canada: from THE POEMS OF DYLAN THOMAS © 1952 by Dylan Thomas. Reprinted by permission of New Directions Publishing Corp.

'A Far Cry from Africa' from *In A Green Night*, © 1962 Derek Walcott. Reprinted by permission of Farrar, Straus and Giroux. All Rights Reserved.

'sorrow song' from *How to Carry Water: Selected Poems*. Copyright © 1988 by Lucille Clifton. Reprinted with the permission of The Permissions Company, LLC on behalf of BOA Editions Ltd., boaeditions.org.

'Home' © 2022 Warsan Shire. From *Bless The Daughter Raised By A Voice in Her Head: Poems*. Used by permission of Random House, an imprint and division of Penguin Random House LLC. All rights reserved.

'Death of a Financier' © 1950 Stevie Smith. From *Collected Poems of Stevie Smith*, reprinted by permission of New Directions Publishing Corp.

'Scotland, you're no mine' © 2019 Hannah Lavery. Reprinted with the permission of the author.

'The Incandescence of the Wind' from *An African Elegy*, Jonathan Cape, 1992. Copyright © Ben Okri 1992. Reproduced by permission of Ben Okri c/o Georgina Capel Associates Ltd., 29 Wardour Street, London, W1D 6PS.

Faiz Ahmed Faiz, 'A Prison Daybreak' (Translated). Reprinted from *The Rebel's Silhouette: Selected Poems*. © 1995 Agha Shahid Ali. Published by the University of Massachusetts Press.

'Der fremder in der fremd' © 2022 Irena Klepfisz, from *Her Birth and Later Years: New and Collected Poems, 1971-2021*. Published by Wesleyan University Press. Used by permission.

'Greetings to the People of Europe!,' original Amharic text © Alemu Tebeje. From *Songs We Learn From Trees*, translated by Chris Beckett and Alemu Tebeje. Carcanet Classics, Manchester, 2020.

'The Jumper', Caroline Smith, *The Immigration Handbook* (Seren) 2016.

'From Moss Side: For Morris' © Carla Henry. This poem originally appeared in the *Morning Star*. Reprinted with the permission of the author.

'Peterloo: Estimated Wrap 19.30' © 2018 Kate Rutter. Reprinted with the permission of the author. Kate Rutter is an actor, poet and activist based in Sheffield.

'Please Call Me by My True Names' © Thich Nhat Hanh. From *Call Me By My True Names*, Parallax Press, 1999.

'The Horses,' © Edwin Muir. From *The Collected Poems of Edwin Muir*. Faber and Faber, 2014.

'More Time' © 1998 Linton Kwesi Johnson. Reprinted by kind permission of LKJ Music Publishers Ltd.

'Welling' from *The Kids*, © 2021 Hanna Lowe. Reproduced with permission of Bloodaxe Books.

'Free Flight' from *The Essential June Jordan*, edited by Jan Heller Levi & Christoph Keller, Copper Canyon Books, 2021. © 2021, 2023 June M. Jordan Literary Estate Trust. Used by permission. junejordan.com.

'Warning, When I am Old, I Shall wear Purple' © 1992 Jenny Joseph. From *Selected Poems*, Bloodaxe Books, 1992. Reproduced with permission of Johnson & Alcock Ltd.

YE ARE MANY